PRAYING LIKE JESUS

Praying Like Jesus

What The New Testament Teaches About Prayer

Gary Holloway

www.covenantpublishing.com

Covenant Publishing
P.O. Box 390 Webb City, Missouri 64870
Call toll free at 877.673.1015

Printed and Bound in the
United States of America

International Standard Book Number 1-892435-08-X

DEDICATION

To Mary Alice Holloway,
an answer to prayer.

Table of Contents

INTRODUCTION

You're hurtling down a rain-swept road at fifty miles an hour. Sideways. Your car is completely out of control and the car stalled in your lane looms closer with each passing second. Time seems to stand still as you realize you will crash. What do you do? Even if you've never been to church and aren't sure you believe in God, in those desperate out-of-control seconds, you pray.

Everybody prays. Well, most everybody. According to a recent poll, less than 50 percent of Americans belong to a church, fewer attend regularly, but over 90 percent still pray. One might think prayer is a natural, universally human phenomenon. If prayer comes naturally, then why should we have to learn to pray?

There is prayer, and there is biblical prayer, just as there is worship and biblical worship. Human beings are incurably religious. They will worship trees, idols, money, success, and happiness. Not all worship is to the one true God. Not all prayer is prayer to him. Even we who worship that one God must worship in ways that please him. So, too, not all prayer addressed to God is pleasing to him.

So how does one learn to pray? We learn from people of faith. For most of us it was faithful parents who first taught us to pray. I still fondly recall those childhood lessons – folding the hands together, bowing the head, and saying, "God is great, God is good. . ." or, "Now I lay me down to sleep." I grew beyond those childhood prayers and learned more from other church members about how to pray. I learned from Peggy Cofield, who taught me in Sunday School. Roger McKenzie, our first preacher and countless others whose names I have forgotten taught me how to bow before God and humbly commune with him. From my family and from my church I continue to learn how to pray.

We learn to pray from people of faith, not only from those in our own time, but also from the faithful throughout the ages. To hear the early disciples at prayer is to learn how to pray. But one above all is our teacher. It is Jesus, who answers his disciples' request, "Lord, teach us to pray."

One way Jesus teaches us to pray is through the New Testament. This book is an examination of what the New Testament says about prayer. We will not look at every passage on prayer, but only at the major prayer texts in ther New Testament order. I hope my comments illuminate these passages, but if not, don't let them get in the way. God promises that his word will not return to him empty. If you will hear that word, he is sure to bless you.

This book is intended to change your life. Its intention is to force you to read what the New Testament says on prayer. Not only to read, but to reflect. Not only to reflect, but to pray. And if you pray, your life will change. You can read this book in various ways. You may read it privately, with another Christian, in a small group Bible study, or in a class at church. However you read it, my prayer is that this book will help you and your church to rediscover the habit of prayer and to learn what Jesus and the early church knew, that true power comes only through prayer. Remember that Jesus' first disciples asked him, "Lord, teach us to pray." He still teaches his followers if we will learn.

CHAPTER ONE

OUR FATHER IN HEAVEN: JESUS' TEACHING ON PRAYER (I)

It's midnight. There's a knock on the door. You stumble out of bed to find a police officer there. Your two sons have been in an accident. Both are dead.

How do you pray?

You go with your Dad to the doctor. Dad is 62 and in good health, but lately he's been acting strange. The diagnosis: Alzheimer's disease.

How do you pray?

Another day begins. You get up at the same time, wash the same face, get in the same car, and go to the same job. You have a great family, a good career, a fine church. Life should be wonderful, but you feel empty inside.

How do you pray?

These are not hypothetical situations. I know the people who have been in these circumstances. So do you. Perhaps you're going through them right now yourself. When hurt, shocked, and confused, we know prayer can help, but sometimes we can't bring ourselves to pray. We don't know how.

In times like these we appreciate the plea of Jesus' first disciples, "Lord, teach us to pray" (Luke 11:1). Their cry is ours. For in every trial and every joy in life we can turn to God in prayer. Jesus himself shows us the way, if we will just slow down, stand still, and hear his voice.

Pray in Secret (Matthew 6:5-6)

In Matthew almost all of Jesus' teaching on prayer can be found in the Sermon on the Mount. The primary point of the sermon is that Jesus' disciples must take care that their righteousness exceeds that of the scribes and Pharisees (Matthew 5:20). In Matthew 6, Jesus explains what that higher righteousness means in terms of outward acts of worship – giving alms, praying, and fasting. Jesus commends these acts of righteousness or piety, but to exceed the practices of the Pharisees, one must do these acts for God, not for the praise of others.

Jesus gives two warnings on prayer. First he warns against praying publicly to be seen by others:

> And whenever you pray, do not be like the hypocrites; for they love to stand and pray in the synagogues and at the street corners, so that they may be seen by others. Truly I tell you, they have received their reward. But whenever you pray, go into your room and shut the door and pray to your Father who is in secret; and you Father who sees in secret will reward you (Matthew 6:5-6).

Christ calls us to a higher righteousness that is, first of all, not a showy righteousness. As with almsgiving (Matthew 6:2-4), Jesus calls people who pray to be seen by others "hypocrites." This term is the Greek term for "actor," that is, someone who is playing a role. The implication here is that the hypocrites may not be completely insincere. While they may truly believe in God and may be truly praying to him, the problem is they are not praying to him *alone*. Like actors they are aware of their audience, of those in the synagogue or streets who hear them. It is this audience they primarily wish to please; so, Jesus says, they have already received their reward. The approval or applause of those around them is the only answer their prayers will get. They may think they are praying to God, but in truth they have another audience.

By contrast Jesus tells us to have an audience of one. "Go to your room, shut the door, and pray to your Father in secret." The word translated "room" here is literally the "storeroom," the locked room in the house where valuables are kept. To pray in the storeroom is the exact opposite of praying on the street corner; here no one but God will hear your prayer. If God alone is the audience for our prayers, then his applause is all we hear. What is more important, he alone hears our prayers, for he alone is able and willing to answer.

This command to "pray alone" is not a condemnation of all public or group prayer. Many Scriptures speak of the importance of prayer in public worship and the power of praying with our Christian brothers and sisters. The Lord's prayer itself addresses God as our Father, implying that it was a group prayer. But there is a strong warning here about public prayer. When leading prayer or praying with others in a small group, we must consider the thoughts and feelings of those around us; after all, we are praying with them. But we must never forget that we are praying to God. It is God alone we address. It is God alone who answers prayer. It is God alone who gives our reward.

Don't Babble (Matthew 6:7-8)

Having warned his disciples against praying like hypocrites, Jesus next warns them about praying like pagans: "Whenever you pray, do not heap up empty phrases as the Gentiles do; for they think they will be heard because of their many words. Do not be like them, for your Father knows what you need before you ask him" (Matthew 6:7-8).

Repeated prayers and persistence in prayer are not condemned here. Jesus commends such prayers in other passages. Neither do his words here condemn the use of model or written prayers, since the Lord's Prayer immediately follows this. What he condemns is a "magical" view of prayer. To many pagans, prayers were much like magical incantations. What mattered was not the relation of the worshipers to their gods, but the repeated recitation of the right phrases.

To Jesus, this type of prayer is complete nonsense. The phrase "heap up empty phrases" implies to babble meaninglessly. If such prayers are worthless when made to a pagan god, how much more are they an affront to the living God? Scripture clearly says we should not attempt to manipulate God. He is the sovereign Lord of the universe. He knows all, including our every need, and no "magic formula" will compel him to do our bidding.

We need not babble to God for our God is a God of love. He is not an unfeeling Supreme Being that we must fool and manipulate to secure his bounties. Such were the pagan "gods." But the God of the Bible is a loving Father who not only knows our needs, but also promises to supply all we need.

The last phrase of this passage, "your Father knows what you need before you ask him," raises one of the great unanswered questions of the Bible: "If God knows what we need before we ask, then why should we pray?" Some speculate that prayer is simply for us, not for God. In other words, God will give us what we need whether we ask or not, but he knows that the very act of asking helps us spiritually. While there is some truth in this statement (the act of prayer helps one grow spiritually), this cannot be a complete explanation of the purpose and nature of prayer. Other New Testament passages clearly say prayer is a genuine communication with God that affects the mind of God himself. This is the most profound biblical teaching on prayer and it shows clearly the amazing extent of God's love. In prayer we affect the mind of God. God loves us so much, he puts his very will at our disposal.

We must not misunderstand this great teaching. God is not some tyrant who withholds his blessings until we ask. Nor is he a weak God who cannot bless until he hears the "magic words." This is precisely the view that Jesus opposes. He is a loving God who wants to bless. He knows what we need before we ask. But he works in such a way that our will and our prayers somehow cooperate with his will in accomplishing his purposes for us.

So why pray? We could give many answers:

- "Because it works."
- "Because it is commanded."
- "Because Jesus and the apostles prayed."
- "Because we need to talk to our Father."

The Bible really never tells us why we should pray. It just assumes we will. God's children pray to him. Even though he knows our needs, and wants to bless us, we pray. Because he knows our needs, and wants to bless us, we pray.

But how should we pray?

The Lord's Prayer (Matthew 6:9-15; Luke 11:1-4)

In Luke 11, one of Jesus' disciples asks him, "Lord, teach us to pray." In reply our Lord says:

Pray then in this way:

Our Father in heaven,
hallowed be your name.
Your kingdom come.
Your will be done,
on earth as it is in heaven.
Give us this day our daily
bread.
And forgive us our debts,
as we also have forgiven
our debtors.
And do not bring us to the time
of trial,
but rescue us from the
evil one.
(Matthew 6:9-13)

We know this prayer variously as the "Our Father Prayer," the "Lord's Prayer," or the "Model Prayer." By whatever name, it is the best known prayer among Christians and until recent years was known by practically everyone in the Western world. In light of Jesus' words about empty babbling, it is ironic that this prayer has been repeated countless times in the history of Christianity. No doubt most who pray the prayer are sincere and realize the significance of the words they speak, but often the very familiarity of these words and the rote way in which we say them make it difficult for us to pray this prayer with the power Jesus intended.

So what new thing can one say about the Lord's Prayer? Dozens of books have been written on these few words. Any study of prayer in the New Testament has to start here, but since we know these words so well, what more can we learn about them?

Perhaps little. And yet we must try. By looking again at the familiar phrases of this prayer, perhaps we can recover some of its power and realize anew why this model prayer has stood the test of time.

Note the address of the prayer, *"Our Father in heaven."* In this short phrase we have the great paradox of the nature of God. He is our Father. He is near, close to us. He gently cares for us. He knows all our needs. Meanwhile, he is in heaven. He is God, not human. He is the all-powerful Ruler of the universe. He is holy. His ways are not our ways. We cannot understand or control him. By calling God our Father in heaven, we come to him boldly, as we would to our own father, but we also bow face down before him, unworthy to lift our eyes to his glory.

"Hallowed be thy name." We should hold this great God in reverence. Though we draw close to God in prayer, we bow before him, not only when we pray, but symbolically in our whole life. Each moment we must show respect for God.

But there is more to this phrase than mere reverence for God. The name of God is the way God reveals himself to humankind. Remember when Moses at the burning bush asked the name of God and God revealed it to him? God has more fully revealed his name and nature to us in Christ. To pray that God will make his name holy is to pray that he will reveal himself in our world.

As such, this phrase is similar to the next one: *"Your kingdom come."* This is the pivotal point of the prayer. The Lord's prayer is a "kingdom prayer."To pray that God's kingdom will come is to recognize that the kingdom has already been inaugurated in the church, that God's reign is increasing in the present world, but the ultimate rule of God will not be realized until the end of time. We earnestly pray that God will reign, not only at the end, but today in our lives.

What does it mean for God to reign in our lives? It means we must be one with his will. So we pray, *"Your will be done on earth as it is in heaven."* This prayer has cosmic significance. God's bidding is followed perfectly in heaven. We pray the day will come when it is followed perfectly on earth. But God's will also has a moral force in each Christian's life. If we want God's will to be done on earth, then it must begin with us. Our will must conform to his. Like the angels in heaven, we must always stand prepared to do his bidding.

The remainder of the prayer consists of three requests. The first, *"Give us this day our daily bread,"* seems straightforward. However, in Greek this is the most problematic phrase of the prayer. The word translated "daily" occurs only here in the Greek New Testament. Scholars are not sure what it means. It may mean "daily bread." If so, it is right for us to ask God for the physical needs of life. Most modern Western Christians take daily food for granted. We need to be reminded that the necessities of life, even our meals, are gifts of God, not natural rights or something we earn. "Daily" implies Christians should not hoard their resources, relying on their wealth and not on God. God alone supplies our needs.

A good case can be made that the phrase should be translated, "Give us our bread for tomorrow." If so, God calls us to be farsighted. Planning for tomorrow is today's task. This doesn't mean we hoard our wealth or trust our plans instead of trusting God. It means God wants us to be prudent in our actions. But Jesus also points us to the ultimate tomorrow, to the great messianic banquet to be enjoyed by his followers in the coming kingdom. Thus we pray not just for bread to satisfy our physical hunger, but more important, for what John calls "the bread of life" (John 6:48).

Since we pray to "our Father in heaven," who is a holy God, we cannot pray without a sense of our own sin. We pray for forgiveness of our debts. Here sin is spoken of as a huge debt that we cannot repay, a theme Jesus repeats in the parable of the two debtors (Matthew 18:23-35). In this prayer, as in the parable, the enormity of the debt that God forgave prompts the disciple to forgive his debtors. The past perfect tense of the verb *"as we have also forgiven our debtors,"* is significant. It means not that our forgiving others earns our forgiveness, but that forgiveness of others should be such a feature of the life of the disciple that it is an accomplished fact (see Matthew 6:14-15).

The final request of the Lord's prayer is for God's help in overcoming evil, *"And do not bring us to the time of trial, but rescue us from the evil one."* In our age belief in Satan, "the evil one," seems silly and superstitious to some. But the unbelievable degree of cruelty we see in the world, and the inward knowledge of the depths of our own selfishness confirm what Jesus said. The evil one really is close and powerful.

Though God is vastly more powerful than Satan, he warns his children against overconfidence when facing evil. We ask God to keep us from the time of trial. This is a better translation than "Lead us not into temptation,"since God tempts no one (James 1:13). God, however, does discipline those he loves and he tests our faith to produce endurance (James 1:3). Knowing our own weakness, however, we must not ask for those tests. Instead when Satan tempts or God tests our faith, it is the Father, not ourselves, whom we must trust for deliverance.

In summary, the Lord's Prayer is a kingdom prayer. Subjects in God's kingdom will pray this way. Our king in heaven is also our Father. We pray he will continue to reveal himself on earth so all humanity will reverence his name. We pray his rule will grow on the earth, until that day when all here do his bidding as completely as heavenly beings do now.

But our Father's rule has not completely come, so we need his power in our earthly walk. We pray for our earthly bread, anticipating the heavenly feast. We pray for forgiveness and for the strength to forgive. We pray for escape from trial and for power to overcome the evil one. We recognize that in Christ the kingdom and rule of God has already broken into our world. We pledge to live our lives under his rule. His kingdom is here! And we anticipate the day when he rules over all, when every knee bows before him.

In this way the Lord's Prayer is a model for all Christian prayer. We do more than simply pray these words or make similar petitions to God. All our prayers are like the Lord's Prayer because we are citizens of his kingdom. All of our prayers must have this same sense of anticipation that the kingdom of this world has become, is becoming, and will become the kingdom of our Lord and of his Christ.

The power of the Lord's Prayer recently overwhelmed me. I preached the funeral of a devout Christian woman who gave freely to others. The most touching moments of the service were not the hymns, the readings, or my own poor attempts at eloquence. No, the most comforting and uplifting moments were when the entire congregation spoke aloud the Lord's Prayer. This Christian woman requested this at her funeral and experiencing those words together brought those who loved her closer to each other and to God.

Let us never be hesitant to approach our Heavenly Father with these familiar words, words taught us by his Son.

Questions for further thought

1. What are some situations where we are tempted to pray to be seen by others? Does this mean we should not pray for our food in restaurants? What can we do to make sure our prayers are between God and us alone?

2. Recall some familiar phrases you hear often in public prayers. Are these "empty phrases"? What can we do to keep them from becoming so?

3. What are some ways you have seen the kingdom of God come in your life? What are some ways the kingdom still needs to come?

4. Is it easier to forgive yourself or others? What allows us to forgive others and ourselves?

5. What do you usually ask for in prayer? What does that say about your spiritual life?

CHAPTER TWO

LORD, BE MERCIFUL: JESUS' TEACHING ON PRAYER (II)

Learning to pray is like learning to swim. There are two extreme approaches. You can read all about swimming, practice the strokes in front of a mirror, even read the biographies of great swimmers. When you finish all that, there's still one problem. You don't know how to swim!

On the other hand, someone can just throw you in the deep end of the pool. Sink or swim. There's great motivation in this technique, but also a clear danger of drowning.

So also with prayer. We can learn all about prayer and still not pray. We learn to pray by praying. On the other hand, we need coaching to learn to pray as we should.

Jesus is our coach. The Lord's Prayer is a model for us, but it does not exhaust Jesus' teaching on prayer. In Matthew, even before Jesus speaks of secret prayer and gives the Lord's Prayer, he instructs his disciples to pray the most difficult prayer of all – prayer for one's enemies.

Prayer for Enemies (Matthew 5:43-48)

> You have heard that it was said, "You shall love your neighbor and hate your enemy." But I say to you, Love your enemies and pray for those who persecute you, so you may be children of your Father in heaven; for he makes his sun rise on the evil and on the good, and sends rain on the righteous and on the unrighteous. For if you love those who love you, what reward

> do you have? Do not even the tax collectors do the same? And if you greet only your brothers and sisters, what more are you doing than others? Do not even the Gentiles do the same? Be perfect, therefore, as your heavenly Father is perfect.

This, too, is part of the higher righteousness that exceeds the goodness of the scribes and Pharisees. Old Testament laws instruct a Jew in biblical days to treat a foreigner in some ways better than a fellow Israelite. However, most of the scribes and Pharisees in Jesus' time re-interpret this teaching to allow hatred for any enemy. Jesus calls his disciples back to the nature of God himself. God cares for the righteous and unrighteous, he points out, so we also must learn to love even our enemies.

But surely good Christians have no enemies! So we may think, until reality kicks us in the teeth. Don't you know people at work who smirk and roll their eyes every time you mention God or the church? Have you ever been hassled for no reason by some petty bureaucrat? Have friends ever deceived you? Do they spread lies behind your back?

For several years I taught Junior High in a Christian school. On one occasion my wife Deb asked Eric, one of my seventh graders, what he thought of me and my class (it so happened that I had gotten on to Eric pretty severely the day before). "I wish he'd die," he said. Taken aback, Deb reminded him that was not a very Christian attitude. "OK," said Eric, "I just wish he'd fall off a mountain and break his leg."

We may laugh at Eric's honesty, but I wonder if there are adults who feel the same way about us but won't admit it. Sometimes through no fault of our own we make enemies. We shouldn't be surprised. Jesus had them, too. They did more than wish he'd die. They killed him.

So what can it mean to love our enemy? Surely we cannot have warm feelings toward those who do everything in their power to destroy us. Jesus explains what this love means, and what prayer means, by adding, "Pray for those who persecute you." We cannot feel good about someone who inflicts pain on us unjustly. But we can will his good. We can desire that God will bless, not curse, such a person. Such blessing does not mean God accepts these hateful people as they are. We should pray for their repentance. Neither does love for our enemies turn them into friends. We might pray for our persecutors and find that they persecute us even more severely. No matter. We still are to pray for them, because such prayer reflects the nature of the God who loved us while we were his enemies (Romans 5:10).

But how can such a prayer be sincere? How can we have a heartfelt concern for the well being of one who cheats us, calls us names, harasses us, jails us, yes, who even wants to kill us? We can't. But prayer can be effective even when we don't "feel like" praying. It is natural to want revenge against our enemies. But the command of Jesus and the nature of our Father run counter to such feelings. They say, "In spite of your righteous indignation, pray for the good of your persecutor." Though our feelings say otherwise, this prayer can and must be sincere. For the God who loathes our sins, still loves us. And Jesus himself prayed, "Father forgive them."

The Power of Prayer (Mark 9:28-29; 11:20-24)

We turn now to two passages in Mark where Jesus discusses the power of prayer. Mark 9 tells of a father who has a son with an evil spirit. He brings his son to the apostles, but they cannot cast out the spirit. Their inability leads the father to doubt Jesus. "If you are able to do anything, have pity on us and help us," he says. Jesus replies, "If you are able! – All things can be done for the one who believes." Immediately the father of the boy cries out, "I believe; help my unbelief!" (Mark 9:23-24).

Jesus then casts out the demon. His lesson on prayer is found in his reply to the apostles' question. *"When he had entered the house, his disciples asked him privately, 'Why could we not cast it out?' He said to them, 'This kind can come out only through prayer'"*(Mark 9:28-29).

This is a strange reply. By saying "*this kind* can only come out through prayer," is he suggesting that some demons can be cast out without the power of God? I don't think so. He implies that the disciples' had too much confidence in their own power and not enough in the power of God.

An important lesson comes across here for us modern Christians. Too many times we live our lives like those around us, relying on our own abilities– common sense, psychology, self-help, technology, prosperity – to solve our problems. Like these disciples, we may not pray at all, or if we do, we turn to God in prayer as a last resort, when "this kind" of problem (one we can't solve on our own) arises. This kind of last-resort faith is not what Jesus recommends here. True faith calls for us to rely on God through prayer at all times.

The power of prayer is even more forcefully illustrated in Mark 11. Here also Jesus' teaching on prayer is in the context of a miracle. The day before, he cursed a barren fig tree (Mark 11:12-14). The next morning, the tree is withered to its roots. This startles the disciples:

> Then Peter remembered and said to him, "Rabbi, look! The fig tree that you cursed has withered." Jesus answered them, "Have faith in God. Truly I tell you, if you say to this mountain, `Be taken up and thrown into the sea,' and believe that what you say will come to pass, it will be done for you. So I tell you, whatever you ask for in prayer, believe that you have received it, and it will be yours" (Mark 11:21-24).

Faith that can move mountains is a cliché among Christians. However it is a phrase that can be misunderstood. Too many Christians have prayed for mountains in their lives to be moved and they were not. When that happens, we tend to blame it on our own lack of faith. "If only I could believe enough, then God would answer my prayers," we sometimes imagine, but this is not what Jesus teaches. This kind of attitude places the power in our faith or in our prayers, not in God.

Jesus warns against lack of faith when one prays. "Do not doubt in your heart," he says. But this must be understood in the context of all the biblical teaching on prayer. If God does not do what we ask in prayer, it may be because of our lack of faith. Or it may be that we have asked for the wrong thing. Or it may be that it is not God's will to give it to us. Prayer is not a magical formula: ask + faith = mountains moved. Prayer is talking with God, and we must always pray with his nature and will in mind.

While we acknowledge this ever-present limitation on our prayers, still it is clear that the main point of this passage is to urge us to have faith when we pray. Jesus' language here is exaggerated for effect (much like his camel-through-the-eye-of-a-needle language). I don't believe he wants us to move literal mountains, but he does want us to have faith in a God who can do what seems impossible. The mountains of depression, hopelessness, poverty, addiction, and pain may weigh on us more than all the Rockies combined. Yet God can move those mountains. Jesus does not want us to pray just when we are at the end of our rope, but neither does he want us to stop praying even if the rope breaks. Nothing is too great for God. In prayer, we must never doubt his power or his goodness. No situation is too bleak for prayer.

God answers the prayer of faith, but sometimes his answer is seen only through the eyes of faith. If we pray according to God's will, then we believe that even in those times when we cannot see the mountains of difficulty move, God has still given us his blessing.

Persistence in Prayer (Luke 11:5-13; 18:1-8)

God loves us, he wants to bless us, he knows what we need before we ask, yet he wants us to ask. And not just once. He wants us to keep on asking.

> He said to them, "Suppose one of you has a friend, and you go to him at midnight and say to him, 'Friend, lend me three loaves of bread; for a friend of mine has arrived, and I have nothing to set before him.' And he answers from within, 'Do not bother me; the door has already been locked, and my children are with me in bed; I cannot get up and give you anything.' I tell you, even though he will not get up and give him anything because he is his friend, at least because of his persistence he will get up and give him whatever he needs.

"So I say to you, Ask, and it will be given you; search, and you will find; knock, and the door will be opened for you. For everyone who asks receives, and everyone who searches finds, and for everyone who knocks, the door will be opened. Is there anyone among you who, if your child asks for a fish, will give a snake instead of a fish? Or if the child asks for an egg, will give a scorpion? If you then, who are evil, know how to give good gifts to your children, how much more will the heavenly Father give the Holy Spirit to those who ask him!" (Luke 11: 5-13).

In this parable Jesus compares God to a friend disturbed in bed at midnight. One should not press the comparison too far. The friend will not give because of friendship, but he will give to get rid of his disturbing visitor. God is not like the sleepy, bothered friend. He wants to give us good things. We give our children good gifts, even though we are evil people. How much more will the good God give good gifts to us!

So the parable does not picture God as irritated or bothered by our prayers. The point of the parable is persistence. If being persistent pays off when dealing with ill, sleepy, evil men, then how much more will it pay off when we ask of our loving Father. God does not need to be told constantly of our needs to answer us. He knows them already. But we are told to be persistent, perhaps for our own sake, to mold our wills to his.

A clear difference exists between persistence in prayer and the "empty babbling" Jesus warned about earlier. Jesus is not saying that fifty prayers are better than forty, as if God counts rather than listens to prayer. What he says is, "Don't stop praying." He makes this clear in the next parable:

Then Jesus told them a parable about their need to pray always and not to lose heart. He said, "In a certain city there was a judge who neither feared God nor had respect for people. In that city there was a widow who kept coming to him and saying, `Grant me justice against my opponent.' For a while he refused; but later he said to himself, `Though I have no fear of God and no respect for anyone, yet because

> this widow keeps bothering me, I will grant her justice, so that she may not wear me out by continually coming.'" And the Lord said, "Listen to what the unjust judge says. And will not God grant justice to his chosen ones who cry to him day and night? I tell you, he will quickly grant justice to them. And yet, when the Son of Man comes, will he find faith on the earth?" (Luke 18:1-8).

Here again Jesus makes a comparison that seems unflattering to God. God is compared to an evil judge who cares nothing for others, but who will grant justice to a widow simply to get her to leave him alone. Again, we have here a lesser-to-greater comparison. If someone as rotten as this judge will vindicate the widow just because of her persistence, then how much more readily will the God of love grant justice to his chosen ones?

In Luke's day this parable would be good news. Many in the early church had undergone ridicule, imprisonment, and torture for their faith. They had cried to God for justice, for vindication, but he had not yet rescued them. They were losing heart.

For us who live more than nineteen hundred years later, the parable is still welcome news. At times it seems that evil is triumphant in the world. As Christians our lives are quite strange to those around us. They cannot understand why we do not live for the moment as they do. We forgo temporary pleasures – wealth, hedonism, power – because we believe a new world is coming. Yet it appears that the new age has been delayed. Christ has not yet returned, so we are tempted to lose heart. Those around us appear to have more fun, more life, even more sense than we do. They look like realists and we look like dreamers, wishing for a world that does not exist. But we know better. We know the true reality. Yet we long to be vindicated. We want those around us to see that we were right all along. We want every knee to bow before the Lord Jesus.

So we pray and do not lose heart, for we are confident that God will speedily vindicate us. We pray in light of this reality that unbelievers cannot see. We pray knowing the Son of Man comes quickly to grant justice. The question, according to Jesus, is will he find us faithful?

Humility in Prayer (Luke 18:9-14)

If our quick answer to the question above is, "Of course, he will find us faithful" – if we think our salvation is assured because of our righteousness or perhaps even because of our "spiritual" prayers, Jesus warns us in a third parable against spiritual pride in prayer.

> He also told this parable to some who trusted in themselves that they were righteous and regarded others with contempt: "Two men went up to the temple to pray, one a Pharisee and the other a tax collector. The Pharisee standing by himself, was praying thus, `God, I thank you that I am not like other people: thieves, rogues, adulterers, or even like this tax collector. I fast twice a week; I give a tenth of all my income.' But the tax collector, standing far off, would not even look up to heaven, but was beating his breast and saying, 'God, be merciful to me, a sinner!' I tell you, this man went down to his home justified rather than the other; for all who exalt themselves will be humbled, but all who humble themselves will be exalted" (Luke 18:9-14).

Contemporary audiences are apt to hear this parable in a way completely opposite to how people heard it originally. To us the Pharisee is the bad guy from the beginning. When we hear "Pharisee," we immediately think of a "hypocrite." We don't expect God to answer his prayer. By contrast, we know that the tax collectors are companions to Jesus, so they can't be all bad.

Jesus' listeners know better. After all, the Pharisees are those who take God's word seriously. Their whole lives are spent in devotion to him. They keep the law in every detail. They give to the poor. They fast. Their motto is, "God said it; I believe it; that settles it." And they knew how to pray.

On the other hand, tax collectors are traitors. They take hard-earned money from God's people and give it to a pagan government. They care nothing for God or his law, but live only to line their own pockets. For a tax collector to pray is a waste of time.

So this parable must shock those who first hear it, though it fails to shock us. It is unthinkable to Jesus' hearers that God will not hear a Pharisee's prayer, but will listen to a tax collector. But that is precisely what happens. "All who exalt themselves will be humbled, but all who humble themselves will be exalted."

Contemporary Christians cannot hear this parable unless we identify with the Pharisee. Like him, we love God; we want to keep his law; we pray to him regularly. Those who dispise God's law apall as they did the Pharisees. Homosexuals, child molesters, murderers, thieves, corrupt politicians – and we thank God we are not like them. We might even read this parable and thank God that we are not self-righteous like this Pharisee.

Jesus speaks this parable to us. Prayer must never be a time for us to rejoice in our own righteousness. Only One is righteous, the One to whom we pray. We come to this holy God in the filthy rags of our own righteousness. Yes, we are to approach him boldly. Yes, he is our loving Father. But we always come with these words, "Lord, be merciful to me, a sinner!"

Questions for further thought

1. Do you have enemies? If people don't like you, is it your fault or is it because you try to follow God? What are some ways we show love for enemies?

2. What are some examples you have seen of the power of prayer? How about recent examples you have heard or read about that power?

3. Why should we be persistent in prayer if God knows what we need before we ask? Can we nag God into blessing us?

4. Do you ever compare yourself to those in the world? To other Christians? Should we? How do such comparisons affect our prayers?

5. Have you ever kept a prayer journal to remind you how God answers prayer? Did it help?

CHAPTER THREE

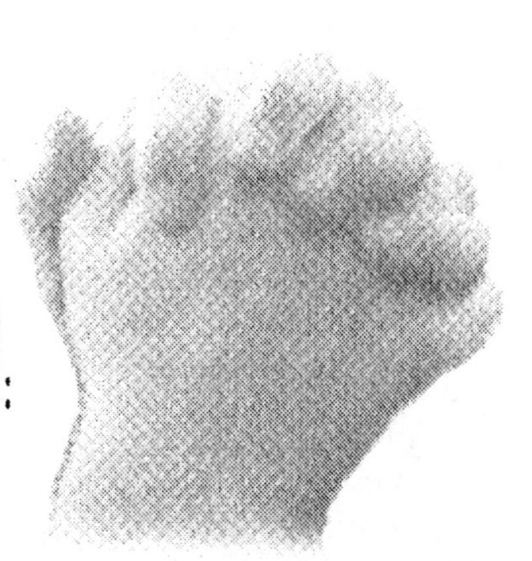

FATHER, I THANK YOU: JESUS' PRAYERS (I)

While we take Jesus' teaching on prayer seriously (after all, he is our Lord), we may tend to overlook the significance of Jesus' own prayers. We may conclude that his prayers are too "spiritual" to be examples for us. Such cannot be the case, for Jesus came to show us how to live in communion with the Father. We may think he never had to struggle to find an answer to prayer, since he had a "direct pipeline" to God. The prayers in Gethsemane prove otherwise. Jesus' prayers are human prayers, the prayers of one who faithfully wrestles with the will of God. We may sometimes simply read past the prayers of Jesus in the Gospels because they occur in stories of his teaching and miracles. In a hurry to get on with the plot of the story, we may ignore the prayers along the way. But we cannot understand the life of Jesus or be his disciple without understanding his prayer life.

Blessing Food (Matthew 14:19; 15:23; 26:26; Luke 24:30)

In the Gospels, whenever Jesus distributes food, he first blesses it. At the feeding of the 5,000 (Matthew 14:19) he "blessed and broke the loaves," and at the feeding of the 4,000 (Matthew 15:36) "after giving thanks he broke them." At the Last Supper, he "took a loaf of bread and after blessing it he broke it, gave it to the disciples, and said, 'Take, eat; this is my body.'" Even the resurrected Jesus when eating with the two men on the way to Emmaus "took bread, blessed and broke it, and gave to them" (Luke 24:30).

It is easy to overlook the blessing of the food in these stories, because the stories themselves are so grand. In the first two stories, Jesus performs astounding miracles: he feeds 5,000 and then 4,000 people with a handful of food, but in each case he takes time to say the blessing. The Last Supper is touching because it is the last time Jesus comes to a table with his men before his death. Still he says the blessing. More significantly he begins a ritual repeated countless times in many places throughout the centuries, a ceremony known by many names including the Eucharist, the "giving of thanks." In the Emmaus story, the blessing of the bread is so characteristic of Jesus that it opens the disciples' eyes to his identity.

But what does it mean to "bless the bread?" Some passages use another term, "to give thanks." When Jesus blesses the bread, he gives thanks to the Father who provides. He not only teaches his disciples to pray for daily bread, but by his example teaches us to be grateful for it. Blessing the bread gives thanks to God and calls on him to bless it for his service. Our food comes from God and is also for God. We eat to live for him.

Prayer for food was once a habit among Christians. Every time we ate we "asked the blessing." Among many Christians, this custom is fading away. Perhaps it is because we eat on the run so often today and seldom have a sit-down meal with our families. But wasn't Jesus as busy, as "on the run" as we? Yet he took time to pray.

Perhaps we neglect prayer for food because it seems so trivial, so trite, so rote. We pray the same prayer every time. After all, the first prayer most of us learned was, "God is great, God is good, let us thank him for our food." Such a prayer may seem childish to us now, so childish that we stop praying at meals altogether. But wasn't prayer before eating a habit of Jesus? Did he not mean it every time?

Or perhaps we do not pray for food because we take it for granted. We've never been really hungry. Our refrigerators, pantries, and supermarkets are stocked. We may have been through some difficulties, but most of us have never had to beg for food. Yet Jesus, who had the power to turn stones to bread, still trusted the Father to provide, and he gave thanks for all he received. We need to restore the habit of thanking God and asking his blessing on each meal we enjoy.

Private Prayer (Matthew 14:22-23; Mark 1:35; Luke 5:16)

Jesus did not confine his habit of prayer to public prayers for food. He also had a habit of private prayer with God. After his public display of power in feeding 5,000, he needed to get away from the crowd to be alone with his Father. *"Immediately he made the disciples get into the boat and go on ahead to the other side, while he dismissed the crowds. And after he had dismissed the crowds, he went up the mountain by himself to pray" (Matthew 14:22-23).* Jesus practiced what he preached. He did not pray for others to see, but spoke to his Father secretly.

Another time, after a long day of healing, Jesus rose early to be by himself to pray. *"In the morning, while it was still very dark, he got up and went out to a deserted place, and there he prayed"* (Mark 1:35). Jesus' popularity as a healer and teacher forced him to make a special effort to get away for prayer. *"But now more than ever the word about Jesus spread abroad; many crowds would gather to hear him and to be cured of their diseases. But he would withdraw to deserted places and pray"* (Luke 5:15-16).

Withdrawing to pray alone was a constant feature of Jesus' life. To him prayer was not just a religious ceremony to be done in the synagogue, not just a custom before meals, and not just a last resort in times of trial. Prayer was the lifeblood of Jesus. Whether late at night or early in the morning, Jesus had to make time to be alone with his Father.

Christians today hear and talk quite a bit about "quiet time." We recognize the value of setting aside a time when we can be alone to pray to God and reflect on his word without being disturbed. But few of us do it regularly. We live in such a busy world where our jobs, our families, and the pressures of modern life do not leave us the luxury of being undisturbed.

But no matter how busy we are, we cannot be busier than Jesus. Who among us is more popular than Jesus? Who has more demands on his time? Do we travel as much? Do we constantly have to deal with crowds? Do we have no refuge, no "place to lay our head?"

Perhaps Jesus had a secret that we fail to grasp. We feel the need and even think it our right to go on vacation to get away from it all. Jesus never took a vacation. But he did make the effort to get away. He made time to pray. I'm not suggesting that it's wrong to take a vacation, but we might be missing the rejuvenating power that Jesus tapped into. If God is truly our Father, then we, like Jesus, must take time alone to talk with him. If we don't, we've missed the point of prayer and the essence of what being God's child is all about. We fail to find the true rest and relaxation that come from being on the mountain with God.

Prayer at the Turning Points of Life

Jesus had a habit of quiet times with the Father, but as a human being he also knew times when prayer was a cry for help and guidance. In the crises of life, in those times of trial that show what a person is made of, Jesus prayed. It is not just coincidence that precisely in these times of prayer and crisis, Jesus is most fully revealed as the Son of God. It is also true that it is precisely such times that test and show our discipleship.

Baptism(Luke 3:21-22)

The baptism of Jesus marks his entry into public life. It reveals him as "the One who is coming," the One for whom John the Baptist prepared the way. In baptism we see Jesus as a man, identifying with our sinful need for repentance. In baptism we see him as the beloved Son of God, pleasing to the Father.

All Christians are familiar with the story of Jesus' baptism. *"The heaven was opened, and the Holy Spirit descended upon him in bodily form like a dove. And a voice came from heaven, 'You are my Son, the Beloved, with you I am well pleased.'"* (Luke 3:21-22).

What we may have forgotten about this familiar story is Luke's revelation that this all happened as Jesus was praying (Luke 3:21).

Prayer and baptism. It seems at first an odd combination. On further reflection, how appropriate it is for Jesus to pray as he begins his public ministry. How appropriate for God to answer his prayer with the Spirit (did not Jesus later say the Father would grant the Holy Spirit to those who asked?). How appropriate for the Father to answer Jesus' prayer with a proclamation of his pleasure in the actions of his beloved Son.

Prayer and baptism. Not an odd combination for Jesus. Not an odd combination for his disciples. After all, isn't baptism a prayer, "an appeal to God for a good conscience, through the resurrection of Jesus Christ?" (1 Peter 3:21). In baptism we pray for the greatest gift of all, our salvation. We pray that God by grace through the death of Jesus will look upon us as his beloved children, and will pronounce himself "well pleased" with us. In baptism, Jesus was pledging his will as one with the Father. He was beginning his public ministry with prayer for the help of the Spirit. In baptism we, too, make a pledge of loyalty to God and receive the gift of the Spirit (Acts 2:38). Our baptism, like Jesus', is a prayer.

Choosing the Twelve (Luke 6:12-16)

All Christians yearn to know God's will in times of decision. Does God want me to marry this person? Does he want me to take this job? To buy that house? To attend that church? The choice is made more difficult when other people are involved. When we must decide who should be promoted at work, who should lead our country, and who should lead our church, we need special wisdom and guidance.

Jesus also needed help from the Father at decision times. One of the most important decisions he made concerned those who would lead his flock after he departed. Whom should he choose to be apostles? No doubt, our choices would be different. The ones he chose were something of a motley crowd: zealots, tax collectors, and fishers. They were uneducated, rough, impulsive men. From a human point of view, none seemed suited for leadership.

But we know the rest of the story. We know that through the power of God and the gift of the Spirit, these leaders, these apostles, became champions of the faith and loving shepherds of the flock. They gave their lives to Jesus, their Lord and Master.

So how did Jesus make such a good decision? Did his insight into people make it easy? Was he just lucky? No. He made this decision through prayer: *"Now during those days, he went out to the mountain to pray; and he spent the night in prayer to God. And when day came, he called his disciples and chose twelve of them, whom he also named apostles"* (Luke 6:12-13).

If Jesus felt the need to spend all night in prayer to the Father before he made this momentous choice, don't we also need to trust the Father with our decisions? Often we make crucial decisions based only on earthly wisdom, on what seems best when we weigh our options. Or worse, we make choices based on an irrational inward feeling, on how things strike us at the moment. Jesus shows us another way – pray about the decision and God will answer you. That answer may be consistent with conventional wisdom and our deepest feelings, or it may go counter to both. There is no simple formula for knowing how God helps in decision making. But Jesus believed in praying through the great decisions of life. So should we.

Revealing Himself as Messiah (Luke 9:19-22)

"Who is Jesus?" is the most important question in history. The way we answer that question fixes our destiny. In Jesus' own ministry, he revealed his identity gradually. Even the Twelve he chose after prayer came to know Jesus' full identity only after a slow process. The first full confession of the nature of Jesus came in response to a question he posed to the apostles during prayer:

> Once when Jesus was praying alone, with only his disciples near him, he asked them, "Who do the crowds say that I am?" They answered, "John the Baptist; but others, Elijah; and still

> others, that one of the ancient prophets has arisen." He said to them, "But who do you say that I am?" Peter answered, "The Messiah of God" (Luke 9:18-20).

This great confession of Peter is the foundation for the church (Matthew 16:17-18) and the foundation of our lives as Christians. To be a Christian is to confess Jesus as the Messiah of God. Note that this greatest of questions ("Who do you say that I am?") and the greatest of answers ("The Messiah of God.") take place when Jesus is praying. Through prayer he reveals himself to the apostles. In prayer we today also see Jesus as he truly is. When we pray, we join him in prayer, and we come to a deeper understanding of his nature as our Savior.

The Transfiguration (Luke 9:29-36)

Soon after his confession of Jesus as Messiah, Peter (along with James and John) saw Christ in all his glory:

> Now about eight days after these sayings Jesus took with him Peter and John and James, and went up on the mountain to pray. And while he was praying, the appearance of his faced changed, and his clothes became dazzling white. Suddenly they saw two men, Moses and Elijah talking to him. They appeared in glory and were speaking of his departure, which he was about to accomplish in Jerusalem (Luke 9:28-31).

Peter was again the spokesman, asking for temporary shelters for Jesus, Moses, and Elijah. No doubt Peter meant this to be a compliment to Jesus, placing him on a par with the great lawgiver and the great prophet. But Luke says Peter didn't know what he was saying (Luke 9:33). Instead, just as at Jesus' baptism, a voice spoke from a cloud saying, "This is my Son, my Chosen; listen to him!" (Luke 9:35).

On the two great occasions where God confesses from heaven that Jesus is his Son, Jesus is praying. It is while Jesus is in prayer that God calls him the Beloved. It is in prayer that he receives the Spirit. It is prayer that glorifies him. Luke tells us that believers have the same avenue to God. In prayer we not only see Jesus, but God recognizes us as he recognized his Son.

Prayer also marks us as children of God. Our clothes may not glisten and we may not meet any prophets, but prayer also transfigures us into the shape of the Beloved Son.

The Raising of Lazarus (John 11:41-44)

The theme of Jesus revealed in prayer carries forward in an amazing miracle story in the Gospels, the raising of Lazarus from the dead. Jesus heard that Lazarus was ill, but he waited two days until news came that he was dead. Jesus then took his apostles to Bethany where he met Mary and Martha, the dead man's sisters. He ordered the stone removed from the tomb, although Lazarus had been dead four days.

> So they took away the stone. And Jesus looked upward and said, "Father, I thank you for having heard me. I knew that you always hear me, but I have said this for the sake of the crowd standing here, so that they may believe that you sent me." When he had said this, he cried with a loud voice, "Lazarus, come out!" The dead man came out, his hands and feet bound with strips of cloth, and his face wrapped in a cloth. Jesus said to them, "Unbind him, and let him go" (John 11:41-44).

So much is in this passage. Again we may overlook the prayer because of the greatness of the miracle. And what a miracle! A man dead four days receives life. But the miracle takes place only through prayer. It looks at first as if Jesus ignores his own teaching about praying for show. After all, doesn't he say he is praying only "for the sake of the crowd standing here"? But no. He is not praying for publicity. What we have here is a public prayer that reflects a previous private prayer, a testimony that gives the glory to God.

Note closely what Jesus says, "I thank you for having heard me." Jesus has already prayed secretly, asking the Father to raise Lazarus. He knows his Father has already answered that prayer. But he prays publicly, not so others will think him pious, but so they may know that the power of the miracle comes from God. "So they may believe that you sent me."

Again prayer reveals Jesus as one sent by the Father.

This passage serves as a commentary on Jesus' own teaching on the power of prayer. No one, not the disciples, not the crowd, and neither Mary nor Martha expect Lazarus' resurrection. Even when Jesus plainly tells Martha, "Your brother will rise again," she misunderstands and thinks the Lord speaks of the resurrection at the last day. No one comes forth from the dead, she thinks. It is impossible. But Jesus does the impossible through prayer.

How often do we fail to pray for the impossible? I have a boyhood friend. At one point we were closer than brothers, but our lives took different paths. I remember as a 15-year-old having long conversations with "Bob" (not his real name) about our mutual faith in Jesus and our excitement in studying the Bible (OK, I'll admit we were strange teenagers). But in later years he began to drink, alienated his family and friends, and became a complete recluse. I tried more than once to talk to him about his relationship to the Lord, but he rebuffed me with laughter or with anger. Eventually (I confess) I gave up on Bob and forgot him in my prayers. He seemed beyond hope of change. Impossible.

But others continued to pray for Bob and an amazing thing happened. Like the demon-possessed man of old, the next time I saw him he was "in his right mind," having returned to the Lord and to the church.

Is there a Bob in your life? One who is as spiritually dead as Lazarus was physically dead? Don't stop praying for them. The God who raised Lazarus by the power of Jesus' prayer can do what cannot be done.

Jesus as a Man of Prayer

Jesus was a man of prayer. He prayed in the ordinary course of life. He prayed for what we sometimes take for granted, for daily food. He made time to be alone with God. But he also prayed during the crises of life, those times that sorely tested his faith. At his baptism, prayed to his Father and received an answer from the cloud. Before he chose the twelve he prayed. Before he asked them to confess him, he prayed. While praying his glory shown forth on the mountain. He prayed for power to raise the dead.

In all this Jesus is our example. We, too, should bless our food. We must make time for secret prayer. We also pray in faith to the God who can raise the dead and do other impossible things. But we believe when we pray we are not only following Christ's example, we are also praying with him and he with us. We pray in his name. And like him we know our Father always hears us.

Questions for further thought

1. Do you always pray before meals? If not, isn't this a good habit to cultivate? Can it become an empty habit? What might prevent that?

2. Do you have a time set aside for private prayer each day? If so, when? If not, what keeps you from this habit of prayer?

3. Is baptism a prayer? If so, how does it relate to the "sinner's prayer" that many ask those outside Christ to pray?

4. In what sense do we see Christ revealed and transfigured in prayer? Do we better understand who he is when we pray?

5. Since Jesus prayed aloud at the tomb of Lazarus, is there a place for Christians to pray to be seen by others? Does this contradict Jesus' instruction that we should pray in secret?

CHAPTER FOUR

NOT MY WILL, BUT YOURS: JESUS' PRAYERS (II)

Jesus had a habit of private prayer. Wouldn't it be great to listen in on one of those prayers? How exciting, how helpful it would be to hear how he spoke to the Father.

Jesus prayed in the crises of life. Wouldn't it be a comfort at times of confusion and decision in our lives to hear Jesus' words as he prayed in pain?

Intercessory Prayer (John 17)

We can hear his words. One chapter in the New Testament, John 17, is an extended prayer of Jesus. This long prayer is, no doubt, typical of the way Jesus prayed secretly to the Father. It also is a prayer of crisis, his prayer after the Last Supper just before his betrayal. Having dismissed Judas the betrayer from the Supper, he plainly tells his disciples, "I am with you only a little longer" (John 13:33). In John, this prayer is Jesus' final prayer before the crucifixion, yet with the cross before him, he prays less for himself than for his disciples.

In the first part of the prayer Jesus recognizes his work will soon be complete:

> After Jesus had spoken these words, he looked up to heaven and said, "Father, the hour has come; glorify your Son so that the Son may glorify you, since you have given him authority over all people, to give eternal life to all whom you have given him. And this is eternal life, that they may know you, the only

> true God, and Jesus Christ whom you have sent. I glorified you on earth by finishing the work that you gave me to do. So now, Father, glorify me in your presence with the glory I had in your presence before the world existed" (John 17:1-5).

Jesus is so dedicated to going to the cross, that he speaks as if the deed is already done: "I glorified you on earth by finishing the work that you gave me to do." He also displays his trust in God's faithfulness, affirming in this prayer that since he has completed the task God gave him to do, God will glorify him. This is an obvious reference to the resurrection. Although Jesus heads to the cross, he prays in faith that God's power will accomplish the impossible, that his horrible death will bring him to life and glory. As Christians take up the cross daily, like him in prayer we must trust the faithful God who brings triumph and glory out of death and defeat.

Even facing death, Jesus thinks not of himself but of his apostles. The bulk of this prayer is for "those whom you gave me" (John 17:9). He has already promised these disciples that he will not leave them "orphaned," but will give them the Holy Spirit to teach and guide them (John 14:18-26). Still he is concerned for the safety of his men, because he knows persecution awaits them.

> I have given them your word, and the world hated them because they do not belong to the world, just as I do not belong to the world. I am not asking you to take them out of the world, but I ask you to protect them from the evil one. They do not belong to the world, just as I do not belong to the world. Sanctify them in your truth; your word is truth. As you have sent me into the world, so I have sent them into the world. And for their sakes I sanctify myself, so they also may be sanctified in truth (John 17:14-19).

Here is the essence of discipleship: God sent us into the world, yet we do not belong in the world. God's word, the truth, sanctified us. It marked us as God's own people and the world hates us for it. But just as Christ loves the world and is sent into it, so we disciples are sent into the world for the sake of Christ.

We learn from these words of prayer. Today we Christians

do not always realize the precarious position we occupy in this world. Too many of us have made peace with this world and feel quite at home in it. In contrast to such "worldly Christians," the true disciple will always face danger from the world. Jesus foresees this danger and prays for God to protect his followers. We also should pray to God for strength and protection from a world that so easily distracts us from the business of discipleship.

These words also teach us about intercessory prayer. Facing imminent death, Jesus thinks not of himself, but of his chosen men. How many of our own prayers, particularly during crises, center solely on our personal needs and wants? We must learn to pray for others. We must pray for their physical needs, for health and food. We must pray for their emotional needs, for their peace and joy. We must pray, as Jesus does, for their spiritual needs, that God will keep them safe from the evil one. We must pray even for our enemies, for those still in the world, that their eyes may be opened to the love of God in Christ.

A boy in our church recently taught me this lesson of care for others. Walt is a typical 5-year old, full of life and smart as a whip. Born with a bone weakness, last month he broke his leg for the fifth time. In a cast and in pain, Walt learned that an older woman in our church, a friend of his, had passed away. "She'll have a new body!" he said with glee. Though his own body had betrayed him, Walt could rejoice with others. In the same way, facing death, Jesus thinks of us.

One could hear Jesus praying only for the disciples of his day. But he also prays for us:

> I ask not only on behalf of these, but also on behalf of those who will believe on me through their word, that they all may be one. As you, Father, are in me and I in you, may they also be in us, so that the world may believe that you have sent me. The glory that you have given me I have given them, so that they may be one, as we are one, I in them and you in me, that they may become completely one, so that the world may know that you have sent me and have loved them even as you have loved me. Father, I desire that those also, whom you have

> given me, may be with me where I am, to see my glory, which you have given me because you loved me before the foundation of the world (John 17:20-24).

We who believe in Christ through the apostles' words are also included in this prayer. Jesus prays for us! Yet, because of the current situation of the church, his prayer is a challenge: he prays that all believers may be one. Sadly, the history of the church has mainly been the history of Christian disunity. Even today, we spend much of our energy focusing on what divides rather than on what unites Christians. If Jesus prays for our unity, then we cannot call him Lord and simultaneously fight with our Christian brothers and sisters.

Christian unity begins with the unity of the Father and the Son. Only by being in union with them are we united with one another. And only in that union will the world know the One whom God sent (John 17:23). A wise Christian teacher once told me that the problem with most Christians is that they are too concerned with being "right." If I care only that I am right and you are wrong, we can never have unity. But if both of us realize that only God himself is ultimately "right," then our focus will be on being close to him. And the closer we get to him, the closer we get to each another. This is the key to Christian unity – we are one only in Christ.

But Christ prays an even more astonishing prayer for us. He prays that we will see him in his glory. Jesus had faith that God will raise him from the dead and glorify him in heaven. This Jesus who calls us to die with him, also prays for us to share in his resurrection and his glory.

Jesus concludes his prayer by speaking of love:

> Righteous Father, the world does not know you, but I know you; and these know that you have sent me. I made your name known to them, and I will make it known, so that the love with which you loved me may be in them, and I in them (John 17:25-26).

In the Lord's Prayer, Jesus prays that God's name will be holy. Here he says he has made that holy name known to his disciples (that name is love). To know God is to know love.

This is the essence of Jesus' prayer for us, that we know the love of God. Jesus, the love of God incarnate, wants to be in us. We must let him in. We pray God's love will fill our lives. We pray Christ will be in us.

Gethsemane (Matthew 26:36-46; Mark 14:32-34; Luke 22:39-46)

Yes, Jesus has faith in the Father's goodness. He trusts God to bring him through death and to glorify him. But he also knows that prayer can change the will of God. Facing an unjust, shameful, and cruel death, Jesus prays for deliverance; he prays to change God's will:

> Then Jesus went with them to a place called Gethsemane; and he said to his disciples, "Sit here while I go over there and pray." He took with him Peter and the two sons of Zebedee, and began to be grieved and agitated. Then he said to them, "I am deeply grieved, even to death; remain here, and stay awake with me." And going a little farther, he threw himself on the ground and prayed, "My Father, if it is possible, let this cup pass from me; yet not what I want, but what you want." Then he came to the disciples and found them sleeping; and he said to Peter, "So, could you not stay awake with me one hour? Stay awake and pray that you may not come into the time of trial; the spirit indeed is willing, but the flesh is weak." Again he went away for the second time and prayed, "My Father, if this cannot pass unless I drink it, your will be done." Again he came and found them sleeping, for their eyes were heavy. So leaving them again, he went away and prayed for the third time, saying the same words. Then he came to the disciples and said to them, "Are you still sleeping and taking your rest? See, the hour is at hand, and the Son of Man is betrayed into the hands of sinners. Get up, let us be going. See, my betrayer is at hand" (Matthew 26:36-46).

In Gethsemane Jesus struggles with the same question that often confronts us – what is God's will for us? We know God's ultimate will is for us to be his sanctified people and live with him in glory. But what is his will for us in time of suffering? God loves us; surely he does not want us to suffer. We are his children; he gives only good gifts to us. However, the Bible makes it clear that pain and suffering can be for our own good. Yes, we are God's children, but "the Lord disciplines those whom he loves, and chastises every child which he accepts" (Hebrews 12:6). But surely not all suffering is God's will. How can we know whether it is or not? Can't God change his mind?

Jesus faces this same dilemma. He has predicted his death and resurrection (Matthew 26:2,32). He knows on one level that it is God's will for him to die on the cross. Yet he has to wonder, "Could God change his mind?" So, grieved and agitated, he prays.

In this time of crisis and decision, Jesus has to face the Father, but he also wants his disciples near. He asks Peter, James, and John to share this burden of grief with him. All they can do is sleep. Often before, Jesus escaped from the disciples to be alone in prayer. This time he needs them to watch with him. But they fail him. He is alone.

Alone, but with his Father. He prays the first time, *"If it is possible, let this cup pass from me."* There still seems to be hope that the Father has changed his mind, that he has found another way, that it is possible for Jesus to avoid the cross. But if the Father wants him to die, Jesus is willing.

After finding his men asleep, Jesus prays a second time. This prayer is different, *"If this cannot pass unless I drink it, your will be done."* Jesus is coming to realize that there is no other way but through the cross. Through prayer, he is learning the will of the Father. Finding the apostles asleep again, he prays a third time before he sees the betrayer coming. Now he is ready for the crisis, for the cross, because he has prayed for the will of his Father.

We will probably never face this same situation. It is unlikely we will be called to give our lives in obedience to God's will. But many early Christians faced their own Gethsemanes. The night before they were to be burned alive, or thrown to lions, or crucified like their Lord, they must have prayed this prayer, "Please let this pass, but your will be done." God willed that many be martyred, but through his grace in Christ he gave them strength to be faithful to death, just as he strengthens Jesus in the garden.

We may not be called upon to die, but in another way, we Christians today do face our own Gethsemanes. We may not struggle with a horrible death for our faith, but we do face the battle of our will and God's will. Our problem may not be knowing God's will, but doing it. Like Peter, we find our spirit willing, but our flesh weak. The cup we may want to pass is not persecution, but responsibility.

We know God's will is for us to overcome temptation, to live for others, to do what is right. We know he calls us to be faithful to our spouses, to nurture our children, to care for strangers, and to love the church. Unlike Christ, we agonize not over God's will, but over our own. But if he had the courage to go to a literal cross, then through him we can find the courage to take up the daily cross of obedience to the Father's will.

On the Cross (Matthew 27:45-46; Luke 23:34; Luke 23:46)

Prayer and the cross. They seem to go together. It is no surprise to find Jesus talking with his Father at the great crisis of his life. The first prayer from the cross is a poignant cry. "About three o'clock Jesus cried with a loud voice, '*Eli, Eli, lama sabachthani?*' that is, 'My God, my God, why have you forsaken me?" (Matthew 27:46).

This is a cry of pain. The pain is so intense, the scene so memorable, that Matthew records the very words Jesus spoke in Aramaic. In the past at times of crisis the Father appeared in a cloud to proclaim Jesus as his "beloved Son." Now on the cross he hears nothing but silence from the Father. At times all of us feel abandoned by God. We cry in pain. God truly abandoned Jesus.

This cry is a cry of love. After all, Jesus is not forsaken because of his own sin, but for ours. It is his love for us that drives him to the cross. As Paul later says, "For our sake he made him to be sin who knew no sin, so that in him we might become the righteousness of God" (2 Corinthians 5:21). Because the holy God loved us, he had to turn his back on his own. What greater pain can there be than for God to forsake us? What greater love can there be than to bear such pain for others?

This cry is also a cry of hope. Hope? Yes, for Jesus here is not using his own words, but is quoting the first line of Psalm 22. Jesus knows the Scriptures, so we can be sure he quotes this verse with the entire Psalm in mind. In Psalm 22, David cries to the Lord in pain, but (as in many Psalms) this cry of pain ends in a confession of faith and hope in God. Though the Psalmist feels forsaken, in truth he knows the Lord "did not despise or abhor the affliction of the afflicted; he did not hide his face from me, but heard me when I cried to him" (Psalm 22:24).

Jesus' cry sounds like a cry of hopelessness, but he chooses to quote the first verse of a psalm that ends in hope. Abandoned by his Father, Jesus knows that ultimately God will hear his cry and deliver him. And God does exactly that by raising him from the dead.

In deep pain on the cross, even abandoned by his God, Jesus still thinks of others, even those who are crucifying him. He prays, *"Father, forgive them; for they do not know what they are doing"* (Luke 23:34). Earlier he taught his followers, "Pray for those who persecute you." Here Jesus practices what he preached. What greater example of forgiveness can there be? If while Jesus is dying on the cross, he can pray for the very people who condemned him, spat upon him, and drove the nails home, can we fail to pray for those who wrong us? Against whom do you still hold a grudge? Who is out to get you? Who belittles, ridicules, and ignores you? What is their name?

Pray for them.

Jesus' last prayer is exactly what we would expect – a prayer of trust in the Father's will. *"Then Jesus, crying with a loud voice, said, 'Father, into your hands I commend my spirit'"* (Luke 23:46).

A few weeks ago I stood beside the hospital bed of a Christian sister who faced brain surgery. I told her we were praying for her complete recovery and hoped she'd be back in church soon. She replied, "I appreciate that," then looking me in the eye she calmly said, "but if things don't work out,

I'm ready to go." Two weeks later she died.

Such faith awes and humbles me, for I cannot say with my whole heart, "I'm ready to go." But my prayer, our prayer, is that we have her faith and the faith of Jesus: "Into your hands I commend my spirit." In other words, "I'm ready to go." Some day each of us will face death. May we face it this way, trusting the Father with our future.

In Jesus' Name (Matthew 18:19-20; John 14:13-14, 15:16, 16:23-27)

So how should Christians pray? To learn to pray we must look to Jesus. We must follow his great teachings on prayer. We must learn to pray as he prays, to have a habit of private prayer and to trust God in prayer during the crises of life. But that is not all. We also pray in the name of Jesus (Matthew 18:19-20; John 14:13-14; 15:16; 16:23-27). "In Jesus' name" is not some magical phrase we use to end our prayers. To pray in his name means we pray with the authority of Jesus. When we pray, he prays with us. Our prayers are his and his prayers ours.

As we turn to the rest of the New Testament to look at the prayers of the early church, let us remember that these, too, are the prayers of Jesus. When the disciples pray, he prays with them. As we learn to pray from them, we also are learning to pray like him.

Questions for further discussion

1. How much of your prayer life is spent interceding for others? Do you pray more for others than yourself? Should we pray more for their physical or their spiritual well being?

2. Jesus prayed for unity among his followers. Do we? Can we pray for unity without working toward it? What are some practical ways we can promote unity?

3. What does it mean to pray, "God's will be done"? When was the last time you had trouble accepting God's will?

4. Have you ever felt forsaken by God? Was Jesus' cry of being forsaken a prayer? How can we pray when we feel forsaken?

5. How do we commit our spirits to God in prayer? Is this similar to whatJesus did on the cross?

CHAPTER FIVE

THEY DEVOTED THEMSELVES TO PRAYER: PRAYER IN ACTS (I)

Acts is the story of the church. The story of the church is the story of prayer. Yet Acts of the Apostles is one of the neglected books of the New Testament. When we do study it, we generally concentrate on the conversion stories or on Paul's missionary journeys. But Acts is a much richer book, containing a wealth of insight on what it means to be a community of disciples, including examples of how to pray.

We must mine that wealth. To do so, one must keep two facts about Acts in mind. First, the theme of Acts is being witnesses for Jesus. At the beginning of the book, Jesus appears to the apostles for the last time saying, "You will receive power when the Holy Spirit has come upon you; and you will be my witnesses in Jerusalem, in all Judea and Samaria, and to the ends of the earth" (Acts 1:8).

This apostolic witness through the power of the Spirit carries on in spite of fierce opposition. Not only the apostles, but other disciples "went from place to place, proclaiming the word" (Acts 8:4). No threat could stop their witness, for their courage came not from themselves but from the Father, Son, and Spirit through prayer.

The second important fact to remember about Acts is that it is the second volume in a two-volume work. Luke tells the story of Jesus in his Gospel and the story of the church in Acts. But the story is really one. Acts is like a fifth gospel, displaying Jesus' actions on earth after his ascension. It is Jesus who sends the miracles and the Spirit at Pentecost. Jesus' name is called at baptisms and at healings. Jesus did not end his work at Calvary, or at the empty tomb, or even at his ascension. He is coming again, the Scriptures assure us, but in a sense he never left. He lives in the world through the church.

As we watch the church pray in Acts, we are watching Jesus pray as well. Luke goes to great pains to explain that the church does what Jesus did. As the disciples bear witness to Jesus, they become one with him. His ministry becomes their ministry; his prayers become their prayers.

Constancy in Prayer (Acts 1:14; 2:42; 6:4)

Since the church is to pray like Jesus prayed, we are not surprised to find them constantly at prayer. In Luke, Jesus has a habit of withdrawing alone for prayer. In Acts, the disciples have the same habit of prayer. *"They were constantly devoting themselves to prayer, together with certain women, including Mary the mother of Jesus, as well as his brothers"* (Acts 1:14).

In Acts 1, the disciples are a confused lot, still expecting Jesus to set up an earthly kingdom (1:6). At the ascension we find them gawking toward heaven, unsure of what to do (1:10). They are a small group, about 120 persons, not much to build a worldwide movement on. They have not yet received the power of the Spirit. But in spite of their limitations, these disciples have learned at least one thing from their Master – they need constantly to pray.

This habit of prayer continues after Pentecost and spreads to the new disciples. *"They devoted themselves to the apostles' teaching and fellowship, to the breaking of bread and prayers"* (Acts 2:42). The converts on Pentecost were all Jews. They knew their prayers, but they still needed to learn to pray as Jesus prayed. Many of these converts knew little of what Jesus had taught the apostles. Imagine their excitement at hearing the Lord's Prayer for the first time. Imagine Peter, James, and John telling of the prayer, the glory, the visitors, and the voice at the Transfiguration. Imagine how shocked they were to learn that they must pray even for their enemies. These converts learned to pray from Jesus. They learned to devote themselves to prayer.

The apostles were more than teachers of prayer. They also devoted themselves to prayer. When a dispute arose in the church concerning the distribution of food to widows, they appinted seven men to take care of this problem so the apostles could "devote themselves to prayer and to serving the word" (Acts 6:4). Caring for the poor is certainly an act close to the heart of God, but so is prayer. The early church neglected neither.

Most modern churches have an abundance of ministries – worship ministries, youth ministries, older-adult ministries, sports ministries, ministries to the poor, the homeless, and the sick. What about a ministry of prayer? What if some in the church were designated "prayer ministers" who, like the apostles, would devote themselves to prayer. This would revolutionize the church.

What power these early Christians had! What fellowship! What was their secret? Loyalty to Jesus? Of course. The power of the Spirit? Yes. But they also knew the secret of prayer. The early church was a praying church. That was the source of their power. If we are to recapture their faith and their witness, we must learn to be constantly in prayer.

Prayer During the Challenges of Faith

Like Christ, the early Christians prayed during times of crisis. Although constant in prayer, they realized they especially needed God's blessing and guidance at other critical moments.

Choosing Workers (Acts 1:23-26; 6:1-6; 13:1-3; 14:23) The church needs guidance when selecting leaders. Today we tend to choose leaders for the church because of their leadership in the wider community. If they are successful business leaders, we assume they will be good church leaders. In most churches the congregation has a loud voice in selecting leaders. No politics is quite like church politics. The process sometimes even degenerates into a democratic one – the candidate who gets the most votes wins.

But the church is not the world and church leaders are to have a different authority than worldly leaders. The early church in Acts knew the loudest voice in choosing leaders must not belong to the congregation but to Christ. They sought his voice in prayer.

Even before Pentecost, the 120 disciples had an important decision to make about who should take Judas' place as an apostle? They proposed candidates based on specific qualifications, but the final decision they left to Jesus.

> So they proposed two, Joseph called Barsabbas, who was also known as Justus, and Matthias. Then they prayed and said, "Lord, you know everyone's heart. Show us which one of these two you have chosen to take the place in this ministry and apostleship from which Judas turned aside to go to his own place." And they cast lots for them, and the lot fell on Matthias; and he was added to the eleven apostles (Acts 1:23-26).

This decision was a crucial one. The full number of the apostles had to be complete to set the stage for Pentecost. To be an apostle was an awesome responsibility, for they were to be witnesses to Jesus throughout the world.

But the disciples did not make this important decision. Jesus did. Just as he had chosen the original Twelve, it is Jesus who picked Matthias. The disciples were unqualified to make this choice. Jesus alone knows the heart. So they prayed and cast lots. The lot fell on Matthias. He became one of the Twelve.

What are lots? They were probably stones of different color, shape, or marking. These stones are placed in a receptacle, probably a bag, and then they shook the bag throwing or "casting" a lot. Here there were two stones, a Joseph lot and a Matthias lot, in the bag. Matthias' lot was thrown.

Why don't Christians cast lots today? I'm not sure. Perhaps we associate it with chance, superstition, or magic. The Bible never makes these associations when the lot is cast in prayer. To cast lots is to leave the decision to the Lord. As one Proverb attests, "The lot is cast into the lap, but the decision is the Lord's alone" (Proverbs 16:33). The real reason we are reluctant to cast lots today may be that we trust our own judgment more than we trust the Lord's.

However, there is a good reason for not casting lots. The choosing of Matthias is the last time this practice is mentioned in the Bible. On Pentecost, the Holy Spirit comes upon the apostles and is promised to all who repent and are baptized (Acts 2:38). In the rest of Acts, leaders are chosen not by prayer and lots, but by prayer and the Spirit. In Acts 6, the church chooses leaders "full of the Spirit," the apostles appoint these seven men by prayer and the laying on of hands (6:1-6).

Later, in Antioch, during prayer and worship the Spirit chooses Barnabas and Saul for special work. They also go on their mission with prayer, fasting, and the laying on of hands (Acts 13:1-3). On their mission, Paul and Barnabas in turn appoint elders in each church "with prayer and fasting" (Acts 14:23).

We must learn from these early Christians. The church today needs strong leaders, strong servants who will give their lives in witness to Jesus. One important thing a church can do is choose good leaders. We must make this choice based not on earthly standards, but on the will of God. We know his will through Scripture and through prayer. If Jesus prayed all night before selecting the apostles, if the apostles prayed as they cast lots for Matthias, if the early Christians prayed when choosing and appointing leaders, then we also must pray that the decision concerning Christian leaders will be the Lord's alone.

Although these passages primarily focus on prayer in selecting leaders, they mention two practices connected with prayer in passing. One is fasting. I need to say much about fasting. The practice is found throughout both Testaments. There are many books on the subject. Here we note only that fasting relates closely to prayer. Fasting does much for the body and the soul, but one thing it does is to clear our minds so we can concentrate on the source not only of our food, but of our life – God alone. In fasting and prayer, one comes to know the Father's will.

Another practice associated with prayer is the laying on of hands. At first this custom seems to signify that some power inherent in the apostles passed on to others. However, prayer always accompanies the laying on of hands. No human has power in himself to appoint someone to a position of leadership in the church. Laying on of hands, with prayer, signifies that the appointment is not manmade, but made by God alone. He chooses leaders. He appoints leaders. Their power comes not from human authority, but from God and Christ, through the Spirit.

During Persecution (Acts 4:23-31; 12:12-17; 16:25-34; 7:59) The Christians in Acts faced great persecution. They lived from moment to moment knowing they might have to suffer and even die for their witness to Jesus. The word martyr comes from the Greek word "witness." In their moments of pain, it was prayer that sustained these early disciples.

The first mention of opposition is in Acts 4 where Peter and John are arrested for healing a lame man in the name of the resurrected Jesus. The Jewish authorities order them not to preach in the name of Jesus. They reply, "We cannot keep from speaking about what we have seen and heard" (Acts 4:20). Astounded by their boldness, the authorities threaten them and release them. After their release, Peter and John find the rest of the disciples, recount their story, and then the assembled Christians pray:

> "Now, Lord, look at their threats, and grant to your servants to speak your word with all boldness, while you stretch out your hand to heal, and signs and wonders are performed through the name of your holy servant Jesus." When they had prayed, the place in which they were gathered together was shaken; and they were all filled with the Holy Spirit and spoke the word of God with boldness (Acts 4:29-31).

What would our prayer be in a similar situation? If imprisoned and commanded to speak no more of Jesus, would we pray for safety? Would we ask God to change the hearts of the officials? Would we ask for persecution to cease? The disciples ask for none of these. They pray for one thing – for boldness to speak God's word. They pray not for an easier path, but for the courage and power to walk the path Jesus walked.

And they are answered! The house shakes, the Spirit fills them, and they do speak with boldness. Today's church needs shaking. Today's church needs boldness. We face little persecution for our faith, yet our Christian witness is tentative and apologetic. We believe in Christ, but we don't want to "force that belief on others." Many Christians have bought into our culture's teaching that one faith is as good as another. We have abandoned, or at least we apologize for the exclusiveness of Christianity – the truth that no other name but Jesus can save. We need courage to speak what we have seen and heard, to proclaim the Good News of Jesus. We need the courage that comes only through prayer.

But the Father not only grants courage in persecution, he also can deliver us from evil. In Acts 12, Herod throws Peter in prison, intending to have him executed. Many disciples meet at the house of Mary, the mother of John Mark, to pray for Peter's release. God hears their prayer and sends an angel to free Peter. Peter then comes to Mary's house:

> When he knocked at the outer gate, a maid named Rhoda came to answer. On recognizing Peter's voice, she was so overjoyed that, instead of opening the gate, she ran in and announced that Peter was standing at the gate. They said to her, "You are out of your mind!" But she insisted that it was so. They said, "It is his angel." Meanwhile Peter continued knocking; and when they opened the gate, they saw him and were amazed. He motioned to them with his hand to be silent, and described for them how he was brought out of the prison (Acts 12:13-17).

The disciples' lack of faith is almost humorous. They prayed for Peter's release, but they don't believe it when he raps on their door. Still they do have enough faith to pray, and God answers them more quickly than they can imagine.

This story illustrates the power of God and the power of

prayer. God grants courage to the persecuted, but if he wills, he can remove the persecution. It is always right to pray "deliver us from evil," if we also pray "your will, not ours, be done." God miraculously delivers Peter and later delivers Paul and Silas from prison while they are "praying and singing hymns to God" (Acts 16:25-34). Prayer can do what seems impossible. At times we may be like the disciples at Mary's house, praying when the situation seems hopeless. But we must not fail to pray.

Yet God does not always set the prisoners free. He sometimes wills his followers to give the last full measure of their devotion. These martyrs, these witnesses to Jesus, find strength and comfort in prayer, even at the point of death, just as Jesus himself prayed on the cross. While being stoned to death, Stephen prays the prayer of Jesus: *"While they were stoning Stephen, he prayed, 'Lord Jesus, receive my spirit.' Then he knelt down and cried in a loud voice, 'Lord, do not hold this sin against them.' When he had said this, he died"*(Acts 7:59-60).

The early church was a suffering church. They counted it joy to suffer for Jesus. They prayed for boldness to witness, no matter what the cost. Some even gave their lives for Jesus, praying to him with their last breath.

The modern church, at least in America, is a satisfied church. Fat and happy, we cannot imagine the possibility of martyrdom. The great persecution we face today may be embarrassed looks, caustic comments, and perhaps a cold shoulder or two. But these puny trials are often enough to keep us quiet about our faith.

Only through prayer can we capture the boldness of these early Christians. Only through prayer can we share their trust in a Father who delivers us from all opposition, even from death itself.

Questions for further discussion

1. What are some specific ways today's church can be devoted to prayer? Does your church have a prayer ministry? Shouldn't it? How can you organize one?

2. Does your church spend much time in prayer when selecting leaders? Do we choose our leaders or does Jesus? Who should?

3. Should we cast lots today? What keeps us from it, fear of superstition or lack of faith in God to answer?

4. Should we fast today? What place does laying on of hands have in your church? Should we revive these first-century practices?

5. What is more difficult, to believe God will free Christians in prison or to trust him when he does not release them?

CHAPTER SIX

PRAY FOR ME TO THE LORD: PRAYER IN ACTS (II)

God gives good gifts. Jesus promised that the Father would give the greatest gift, the Holy Spirit, to those who ask. "If you, then, who are evil, know how to give good gifts to your children, how much more will the heavenly Father give the Holy Spirit to those who ask him!" Luke 11:13).

The Giving of the Spirit (Acts 8:14-17)

There is a connection between prayer and the Holy Spirit throughout the New Testament. At Jesus' baptism, the Spirit descends on him while he is praying. Through prayer the Spirit works in selecting church leaders. Later, in the epistles, we will find that the Spirit helps us when we pray, interceding with God for us. So it isn't surprising to find that prayer fulfills Jesus' promise to send his Spirit.

> Now when the apostles at Jerusalem heard that Samaria had accepted the word of God, they sent Peter and John to them. The two went down and prayed for them that they might receive the Holy Spirit (for as yet the Spirit had not come upon any of them; they had only been baptized in the name of the Lord Jesus). Then Peter and John laid their hands on them, and they received the Holy Spirit (Acts 8:14-17).

The power to give the Holy Spirit was not in the apostles, but in God. Only after Peter and John prayed for them did the Samaritans receive the Spirit. We, too, must take Jesus at his word and pray that the Holy Spirit of God will live in us, guide us, and empower us. This is God's greatest gift because it is the Spirit who makes us children of God.

Prayer for Forgiveness (Acts 8:18-24; 9:10-19)

Not everyone understood about the giving of the Spirit. While some mystery always surrounds the coming of the Spirit (like the wind, he "blows where he chooses," John 3:8), one man completely misunderstood the process. His name was Simon and, being a magician, he thought the Spirit came magically through Peter and John. Simon did not grasp the role of prayer in the giving of the Spirit — that the Spirit came from God, not man. Simon offered money to Peter and John to buy the power to impart to others this "magical" miracle-working power.

> But Peter said to him, "May your silver perish with you, because you thought you could obtain God's gift with money! You have no part or share in this, for your heart is not right before God. Repent therefore of this wickedness of yours, and pray to the Lord that, if possible, the intent of your heart may be forgiven you. For I see that you are in the gall of bitterness and the chains of wickedness." Simon answered, "Pray for me to the Lord, that nothing of what you have said may happen to me" (Acts 8:20-24).

He may not have understood the role of prayer in giving and receiving the Spirit, but Simon did understand Peter's threat and his call to repentance. Peter told Simon to pray for forgiveness. Maybe Simon felt unworthy to do so, for he asked Peter to pray to the Lord for him.

Saul is another who prays for forgiveness. He has blasphemed Jesus and murdered Christ's followers. On the way to Damascus to capture more Christians, Saul is struck blind by a bright light and hears a voice from heaven, a voice that identifies itself as 'Jesus, whom you are persecuting." Jesus told him to go into the city and wait for instructions (Acts 8:1-9).

For three days he does not eat or drink. We are told, "He

is praying" (Acts 8:11). We are not told what he prayed, but surely one thing was uppermost in his mind – the need for forgiveness. Saul had thought Jesus a fake, a false Messiah who led people astray. Out of a mistaken zeal for God, he had imprisoned and killed those who spoke of Jesus' resurrection. Now Jesus has appeared to him and he has conversed with the resurrected Christ. Now he knows himself not as a faithful crusader for God's truth, but as a murderer of the faithful, an enemy of the true Messiah sent by God. All that Saul has fought for turns out to be a lie. His life is upside down. No wonder he fasts and prays. How could God hear the prayers of such a sinner?

But God does hear and, he answers. Ananias comes. Saul receives his sight. He is baptized, "calling on the name of the Lord" (Acts 22:16). He is filled with the Holy Spirit (Acts 9:17).

If God hears the pleas of sinners like Simon and Saul, then surely he hears our cries for mercy. Although Saul, later known as Paul, calls himself the chief of sinners, we know better. We know our own sins. We may not try to buy the Spirit, and we may not kill those who witness to Jesus, but we know our own need for forgiveness. Like Simon and Saul, we also pray the tax collector's prayer, "Lord, be merciful to me, a sinner." And like the tax collector, we go away justified, forgiven by our gracious God.

Prayer for Healing (Acts 9:40; 28:7-10)

"It's a miracle!"

Such a phrase scares many of us today. We have seen too many fake miracle workers. Although we are Christians, we may think God worked only in the past and now works only through "natural law." But the same God who worked in Jesus through prayer also worked in the apostles. He's the same God who works his mighty power in us today.

Jesus had promised power to the apostles, power through the Spirit who enabled them to do "many wonders and signs" (Acts 2:43). In the Gospels, these same apostles had trusted their own power and so were unable to heal the boy with a demon (Mark 9:18). In Acts, however, they have learned the lesson Jesus taught them, "This kind can come out only through prayer" (Mark 9:29). Through the power of God, the apostles do the same miracles Jesus did. They can even raise the dead! When a loving disciple named Tabitha (or Dorcas) dies, the church calls for Peter, who raises her from the dead. But like Jesus at Lazarus' tomb, he does so only through prayer:

> Peter put all of them outside, and then he knelt down and prayed. He turned to the body and said, "Tabitha, get up." Then she opened her eyes, and seeing Peter, she sat up. He gave her his hand and helped her up. Then calling the saints and widows, he showed her to be alive. This became known throughout Joppa, and many believed in the Lord (Acts 9:40-43).

Through prayer the ultimate healing takes place. Dorcas arises from the dead. Her resurrection, like that of Lazarus, leads many to believe.

Other healings take place through prayer. Paul, like Peter, does miracles similar to those of Jesus:

> It so happened that the father of Publius lay sick in bed with fever and dysentery. Paul visited him and cured him by praying and putting his hands on him. After this happened, the rest of the people on the island who had diseases also came and were cured (Acts 28:8-9).

Acts makes it clear, then,that healing took place through prayer. Today we have no one with the power of Peter or Paul, but we still pray for healing, and we still have the power that was in Peter and Paul – the power of Jesus. When doctors pronounce a case hopeless, Christians may be reluctant to pray for healing. But we must not doubt the power and goodness of God. When all is hopeless, God can heal. And sometimes he will heal, through prayer.

However, prayer is much more than a last resort. If we only pray when things are hopeless, we miss the point of prayer. And prayer is not magic. God is powerful. He can heal. God is good. He wants to heal. But God is also God. He alone is the sovereign ruler of the universe. His will, not ours, must guide us.

Dorcas is raised from the dead. Stephen is not. Publius's father is instantly healed of sickness. Paul (who healed him) is himself not healed of his thorn in the flesh. Peter is released from prison. James is not, and is beheaded. Acts is not the story of a constantly triumphant church. Prayer is not a sure formula for health, wealth, and success. Yes, we should pray in faith for healing, but we must pray that God's will be done. When we are healed, it is by his power. When we are not, it is still his power through prayer that sustains us.

Acts is careful to make the point that healing power comes from Jesus, not from the apostles themselves. Today some who claim to heal seem to forget the power is God's. But though there are as many "fake healers" as "faith healers," we must not let our cynicism keep us from praying to the true source of health, to our Father in heaven.

For Guidance (Acts 10:1-16, 31; 22:17-21)

"Does God hear the prayer of a sinner?"

I hope so! All of us are sinners. God hears and forgives us when we pray.

"But does God hear the prayer of one who is not a Christian?"

No, if that person has finally rejected Christ. If one rejects Jesus, how can one pray in his name?

"But what about the person who wants to do right, to follow Jesus, but does not know how?"

Ah, that's different. Many in our world have some idea of God, but do not know Jesus. Even in "Christian" America we might find some who know of Jesus and his church but remain confused about how to follow him. What should such a person do?

In Acts we find such a person. His name is Cornelius. What he does is pray for guidance.

> In Caesarea there was a man named Cornelius, a centurion of the Italian cohort, as it was called. He was a devout man who feared God with all his household; he gave alms generously to the people and prayed constantly to God. One afternoon at

> about three o'clock he had a vision in which he clearly saw an angel of God coming in and saying to him, "Cornelius." He stared at him in terror and said, "What is it, Lord?" He answered, "Your prayers and your alms have ascended as a memorial before God. Now send men to Joppa for a certain Simon who is called Peter; he is lodging with Simon, a tanner, whose house is by the seaside" (Acts 10:1-6).

God definitely hears Cornelius' prayers (Acts 10:30). Cornelius sends for Peter, whom God has prepared through a vision (Acts 10:9-16). Peter arrives, preaches the gospel to Cornelius and his family, the Spirit falls upon them, and they are baptized (Acts 10:34-48).

God hears the prayers of all who seek him. If we do not know how to walk with God, we should pray for guidance. God might not send Peter, but in some way he will show us how to serve him. This is true not only for non-Christians, but for believers also. Even the most committed disciples have times when they don't know how to love Christ. None of us understands the way of God perfectly. We come to know his will through Scripture and prayer.

Sometimes our question is not, "How can I serve God," but simply, "What do I do now?" Life is full of decisions, great and small, and in those decisions we must seek the guidance of the Lord. After his conversion, Saul returns to Jerusalem and receives such guidance. He says,

> "After I had returned to Jerusalem and while I was praying in the temple, I fell into a trance and saw Jesus saying to me, 'Hurry and get out of Jerusalem quickly, because they will not accept your testimony about me.' And I said, `Lord, they themselves know that in every synagogue I imprisoned and beat those who believed in you. And while the blood of your witness Stephen was shed, I myself was standing by and keeping the coats of those who killed him.' Then he said to me, 'Go, for I will send you far away to the Gentiles'" (Acts 22:17-21).

This is an important turning point in Paul's life. He wants to stay in Jerusalem and clear his name. He wants his old friends to know that he now follows this Jesus he once persecuted. But the Lord has other plans for Saul. He wants to send him to the Gentiles. In prayer Paul hears Jesus say, "Go."

Like Paul, we make plans. We decide where to live, what job to have, how to spend our time. Like Paul, we may wish to stay when Jesus says go. But Paul heard the voice of Jesus in prayer, and he obeyed. Prayer is not just speaking, it is also listening.

Paul may not be a perfect example for us here. I'm unconvinced that we should expect to fall into a trance when we pray. I'm not sure exactly how Jesus speaks to us in prayer. I have never heard an audible voice, but at times when I have been wrestling with a decision in prayer, I believe he has answered me and guided me. Sometimes, like Paul, his answer is not what I want to hear, but if we ask God for advice, we should be prepared to take it.

Jesus did not leave the church alone. He has not left us alone. If we want to know his will, we read his word. We follow the example of his body, the church. And we seek his voice in the silence of prayer. We are not alone. He guides our lives.

When Parting (Acts 20:36-38; 21:4-6)

Prayer is not always just between our Father and us. We sometimes pray with our fellow travelers on God's way. Prayer with other Christians is touching and appropriate when we part from them. Having left Ephesus after spending three years there, Paul returns to Miletus on his way to Jerusalem. From there he sends for the elders of the Ephesian church, seeing them for what he thinks might be the last time.

> When he had finished speaking, he knelt down with them all and prayed. There was much weeping among them all; they embraced Paul and kissed him, grieving especially because of what he had said, that they would not see him again. Then they brought him to the ship (Acts 20:36-38).

What a heartrending prayer this must have been. Just a few days later, Paul will repeat this scene with the Christians at Tyre (Acts 21:5-6).

Like Paul, we know the church is a family. To leave fellow

Christians is not just parting from friends. It's more like leaving home. But what makes us family is our common Father. It is he to whom we all pray. In prayer we are united with the Father and with each other. No doubt Paul and the Ephesians pray that God will protect them. No doubt they pray to be reunited in heaven, their true home. But in the very act of parting, they are one in prayer. Nothing can separate us from our Christian brothers and sisters. No matter how far away from us they are, in this world or the next, we are one with them in prayer.

A Praying Church

In many ways the church in Acts is a model church. However, these early Christians are not perfect. They bicker and fight. Their faith wavers. In their midst are some hypocrites. But most of them hold firmly to their faith, even in the face of persecution. They are devoted to God and to one another. Most of all, they are a praying church, calling on their Father repeatedly for courage, forgiveness, and guidance. If we are to imitate their faith, we must be praying Christians, completely dependent on God through Christ.

What makes for a good church today? Is the best church the one with the most dynamic preacher? The most programs? The largest attendance? Do we measure a church by the excitement of its members? By the size of its parking lot? By its reputation in the brotherhood?

No. The truest measure of a church is its devotion to God, and nothing reflects that devotion more than prayer. If we lack the spirituality and power of the early church, perhaps our prayer life is the first thing we should change.

Questions for further discussion

1. Should we pray today to receive the Holy Spirit? How do we know that the Spirit is with us?

2. Is there any sin God will not forgive? What is the relationship between repentance, prayer, and forgiveness?

3. What makes us nervous about praying for healing? Do you think God heals miraculously today? If not, why should we pray for the sick?

4. Have you ever prayed with someone when you were about to part from them? What did you pray for?

5. What more can your church do to show it believes in the healing and forgiving power of prayer?

CHAPTER SEVEN

I THANK MY GOD FOR ALL OF YOU: PAUL'S PRAYERS FOR THE CHURCHES (I)

While reading Paul's letters, many Christians skip over his prayers to get to the "good stuff." For some the good part is Paul's deep presentation of Christian doctrine. His letters are full of profound teachings on redemption, the Holy Spirit, the resurrection, and other doctrines. For some the good stuff is Paul's advice on Christian living, his comforting words on love, joy, and peace.

Paul's letters are deep reservoirs of guidance on Christian living and doctrine, but we can miss both the beauty of discipleship and the significance of doctrine if we ignore his prayers. When Paul writes to a church, he usually begins by praying for them. This surely must be more than a mere custom of letter composition. By praying, Paul recognizes God the Father and the Lord Jesus as the true correspondents with the church. Their power called the church into existence. Their love binds the church together. Their Spirit gives the church life.

Moreover, Paul's prayers usually set the themes for his letters. If you want to know what concerns, frightens, and encourages him about a church, look first to his prayers. There you find what is on his heart.

By looking at Paul's prayers for the churches, we can learn to pray as he did for brothers and sisters in Christ – for those in our local congregation, in other churches, and even those far away whom we have never met.

For the Romans (Romans 1:8-12)

Though he knew many in their number, Paul had never visited the church at Rome when he sat to write to them. This was not a church he planted, so one might expect that his letter to them would show less depth of feeling than his other letters. Such is not true.

> First, I thank my God through Jesus Christ for all of you, because your faith is proclaimed throughout the world. For God, whom I serve with my spirit by announcing the gospel of his Son, is my witness that without ceasing I remember you always in my prayers, asking that by God's will I may somehow at last succeed in coming to you. For I am longing to see you so that I may share with you some spiritual gift to strengthen you – or rather so that we may be mutually encouraged by each other's faith, both yours and mine (1:8-12).

Paul's warm affection for the Romans stems in part from his knowledge of their faith. They are so faithful that the whole world proclaims it. Paul prays for them constantly, asking God to bring him to visit them in Rome. The great apostle wants to bring them a spiritual gift, but he also longs for strength provided by their world-renowned faith.

We learn much from Paul's brief prayer for the Romans. He could stress his own authority as an apostle, his power to heal and pass on spiritual gifts. Indeed, he does mention his call to be an apostle, but in his prayer he prays for mutual encouragement. Paul has learned what truly spiritual disciples always know, that no matter how mature in Christ one becomes, one always needs encouragement from faithful Christians. Paul understands discouragement. He endured beatings, stonings, and shipwreck. But when he thinks of these faithful Romans, resolute even in adversity, his spirit brightens.

We may not face persecution as modern Christians, but we do face discouragement. Even (perhaps especially) those who publicly lead the church face disappointment and heartbreak. But those of us who lead, teach and preach, know we usually receive more than we give to our congregations. The examples of ordinary, quiet, but faithful Christians convince us anew of the truth and power of Christianity.

Margaret is such a Christian. A widow retired from a career in college teaching, her health is fragile. She cannot see very well after dark, yet she never misses a church service, although at times she has to get another church member to transport her. If you were to visit our church, you probably wouldn't notice her. She isn't loud and boisterous, but her acts of quiet service, known only to a few, do not go unnoticed by God.

Many Margarets serve the Lord in our church and in yours. Such Christians keep my faith alive. Like Paul, I long to meet more of them. Like Paul, we all should pray for opportunities to meet Christian brothers and sisters who will strengthen our faith as we strengthen theirs.

For the Corinthians (1 Corinthians 1:4-9; 2 Corinthians 1:3-7; 13:7-10)

Was there ever a church as mixed up as the Corinthians? They were proud of their sexual immorality. They were split into quarreling factions. They sued each other in pagan courtrooms. They got drunk during the Lord's Supper. They bragged about their spiritual gifts, but did not know the way of love.

In short, if there ever was an apostate church, it was Corinth. How disappointed Paul must have been when he thought of them. He had founded the church at Corinth and spent a year and a half there trying to shape them into disciples of Jesus. When he left, other teachers arrived claiming to know more than Paul. They ridiculed his authority. And some Corinthians followed these "super apostles" quite readily.

How do you pray for a church like Corinth? My first inclination would be to pray God to pay them in kind, to blast them out of the water as they deserve. That was not Paul's prayer. With all their faults, the Corinthians had received the grace of God. His prayer for them was not one of rebuke, but of thanksgiving.

> I give thanks to my God always for you because of the grace of God that has been given you in Christ Jesus, for in every way you have been enriched in him, in speech and knowledge of every kind – just as the testimony of Christ has been strengthened among you – so that you are not lacking in any spiritual gift as you wait for the revealing of our Lord Jesus Christ. He will also strengthen you to the end, so that you may be blameless on the day of our Lord Jesus Christ. God is faithful; by him you were called into the fellowship of his Son, Jesus Christ our Lord (1 Corinthians 1:4-9).

Thank God the salvation of the Corinthians was not dependent on their ability to be a model church, but on God's gracious act in Jesus Christ. This gracious God gave them their spiritual gifts, faith, and knowledge. This faithful God will present them blameless at the last day.

This does not mean the Corinthians had no reason to repent. In the rest of 1 Corinthians Paul enumerates their shortcomings and calls them back to faithfulness. They must put away selfish divisions. They must have orderly worship. They must live moral lives based on love. But all these things are by God's grace alone, and for that grace Paul is thankful.

How do we pray for the weak, apostate Christian? The temptation is to pray, "Lord, straighten them out!" Such a prayer may have a place. Our brothers and sisters may need God to figuratively hit them between the eyes to get their attention. But in praying for wayward Christians, we must remember that no matter how sinful they are, they are our brothers or sisters in Christ. They, too, are saved by God's grace, just as are we, and it is that grace, which calls them to repentance. Even the worst Christian can be an occasion for us to thank God for his marvelous grace.

The tone of 2 Corinthians differs greatly from that of 1 Corinthians. It appears the Corinthians have repented of many wrongs they committed, so Paul prays for God to console them.

> Blessed be the Father of our Lord Jesus Christ, the Father of

mercies and the God of all consolation, who consoles us in all our affliction, so that we may be able to console those who are in any affliction with the consolation with which we ourselves are consoled by God. For just as the sufferings of Christ are abundant for us, so also our consolation is abundant through Christ. If we are afflicted, it is for your consolation and salvation; if we are being consoled, it is for your consolation, which you experience when you patiently endure the same sufferings that we are also suffering. Our hope for you is unshaken; for we know that as you share in our sufferings, so also you share in our consolation (1:3-7).

Talk about repeating yourself! Paul uses the word *consolation* nine times in these five verses. Why do the Corinthians need comfort? One reason is their sorrow for their sins. Paul wrote a harsh letter to them, calling the sincerity of their faith into question. Even in this letter he urges them to test their faith to see if it is genuine (13:5).

When confronted by sin, the faithful Christian responds with a godly sorrow that leads to repentance. This is more than merely saying you're sorry. To repent is to realize one has offended the holy God and has hurt Jesus himself, the One who died for us. Such sorrow cuts deep into the soul. Only the consolation of God's forgiveness heals the wound.

The Corinthians also need consolation in affliction. If there is anyone who knows suffering and pain, it is Paul. If there is anyone who knows the comfort of God in the midst of pain, it is Paul. As the Father comforted the Son in his agony, so he consoles Paul who then shares the comfort of God with the Christians in Corinth.

I have not faced much physical affliction for my faith, but I have known sickness, pain, and injury. While writing this chapter, I broke my elbow. I'd like to claim some noble reason for my pain, but I broke it playing softball. For the three weeks my right arm was in a cast, I couldn't write, mow the grass, or even feed myself easily. During this time, the church gave me a surprise birthday party, and one brother endeared himself to me forever by cutting my cake into bite-sized pieces. Such was my "great suffering." But as minor as it was, I needed consolation from my fellow Christians and from God, and I got it. In troubles small and great, God is our consolation, and he expects us to console others.

Most of our suffering is not a result of our Christian faith. Suffering for Christ seems far removed from our experience as modern American Christians. For many generations now, being a good church member advanced, not hindered, our standing in the wider community. But the times are changing. We no longer live in a Christian America. In most places, being a dedicated Christian will not help you socially or on the job. In our society Christianity is still tolerable "as long as you don't take it too far." But that is precisely what God calls us to do, to go too far, to give our all to Christ. We don't have to be objectionable to please Jesus, but if we have the mind of Christ and strive to live his life, some will object, perhaps even violently. We, too, may come to know the need for God's comfort in persecution.

We also need comfort when facing loss. While writing this, I participated in the funeral of one of our church members. Russell Cooper had been a faithful leader in our church. A few years ago he had a series of strokes that left him severely incapacitated. Each day for years his wife Myrtie faithfully visited Russell in the nursing home and cared for him. She consoled him with God's consolation. Russell passed away and I was asked to read Scripture and pray at his funeral. Ostensibly I was there to comfort Myrtie, but her example of giving, undying love was the true consolation to all around her.

The Corinthians have lost loved ones, too. Some are beginning to doubt the resurrection. They think they will never see their loved ones again. In 1 Corinthians 15 Paul writes them to assure them that victory will swallow death in victory. As we stood by Russell's grave, I thought of those comforting words.

Suffering, sin, and death – three strong foes of faith. Paul knows the Corinthians may crack under their pressure, so at the end of this letter he says another prayer for them, a prayer for their perfection.

> But we pray to God that you may not do anything wrong – not that we may appear to have met the test, but that you may do what is right, though we may seem to have failed. For we cannot do anything against the truth, but only for the truth. For we rejoice when we are weak and you are strong. This is what we pray for that you may become perfect. So I write these things while I am away from you, so that when I come, I may not have to be severe in using the authority that the Lord has given me for building up and not for tearing down (2 Corinthians 13:7-10).

Paul's final words here sound ominous, but in prayer we find their true intent. Paul is not an authoritarian dictator but a loving father in the gospel. Even if he fails, he wants his converts to pass the test of faith, so he calls on the only power that can make them able to pass. He calls on God in prayer.

Suffering, sin, and death are our foes, too, along with indifference, materialism, and pride. If our faith is to pass the test, we also must rely on God in prayer. And we must pray for each other. If Paul can ask God to perfect a church as weak as Corinth, then we can pray for our weakest brother or sister. And they can pray for us.

For the Ephesians (Ephesians 1:16-19; 3:14-19)

Knowledge is power. At least that is what we are told in today's information age. While he is writing to the Ephesians, Paul prays that they will receive a different sort of knowledge and power.

> I do not cease to give thanks for you as I remember you in my prayers. I pray that the Father of our Lord Jesus Christ, the Father of glory, may give you a spirit of wisdom and revelation as you come to know him, so that, with the eyes of your heart enlightened, you may know what is the hope to which he has called you, what are the riches of his glorious inheritance among the saints, and what is the immeasurable greatness of his power for us who believe, according to the working of his great power (1:16-19).

Knowledge of God is much more than a theological education. I do not want to disparage Christian education. I've been in that business all my life. But knowing about God is different from knowing God. Knowing the Bible is important. We should teach it to our children, take time to study it ourselves, and insist that our ministers get the best biblical education they can get. But book knowledge, even of the best Book, is different from as knowing someone. God surely wants us to learn about him, but most of all he wants us to know him.

I know many things about my wife Deb – her taste in clothes, her favorite color, the foods she likes, her sense of humor. But passing a quiz on her tastes and habits does not qualify me as a good husband or insure a good marriage. What makes our marriage good is that we know each other. We are part of each other. We think and feel together. God calls us to have this intimate knowledge of him. Paul prays the Ephesians will receive not simply intellectual information, but that "the eyes of your heart may be enlightened." Our Father wants us to see him with the eyes of our heart. Can there be more intimate knowledge?

Such knowledge is a gift of God. You and I must strain every nerve to know our Father, but we can only know him as he reveals himself to us. Paul prays that God "may give you a spirit of wisdom and revelation so that you may know him better." If we want to know God better, we need only to ask him. Do you want to improve your Bible study? Then coat your studies with prayer. Knowledge comes through prayer. In prayer we come to know the Father intimately, and in prayer he grants us even fuller knowledge.

Who is this God we know? Paul says he is the God who gives hope, "the riches of his glorious inheritance in the saints." The more we know him, the more we realize what he does for us. When we were hopeless, he gave us hope. When we were orphans, he adopted us and made us heirs. Today our world is low on hope. Cynicism abounds. The things on which we place our hope prove futile – wealth, technology, democracy, family, pleasure, and others. God alone is the source of true hope. His is a true and sure hope, not just a fond wish for things to get better. The more we come to know our Father, the clearer we see the reality of our inheritance. Then we have begun to live with him forever.

Knowledge is power. The God we know is a powerful God. The same power that raised Christ from the dead, that placed him in the heavens, that appointed him head over the church – that same power is at work in us (Ephesians 1:20-23). To know God is to have power over temptation, sin, evil, and Satan. To know God is to have power over every situation we face each day. To know God is to have the power of Christ in us, the Christ who fills us in every way.

Knowledge is power. Paul repeats this in his second prayer for the Ephesians.

> For this reason I bow my knees before the Father, from whom every family in heaven and on earth takes its name. I pray that, according to the riches of his glory, he may grant that you may be strengthened in your inner being with power through his Spirit, and that Christ may dwell in your hearts through faith, as you are being rooted and grounded in love. I pray that you may have the power to comprehend, with all the saints, what is the breadth and length and height and depth, and to know the love of Christ that surpasses knowledge, so that you may be filled with all the fullness of God (Ephesians 3:14-19).

Knowledge of God brings power, but here Paul turns it around, praying that the Ephesians will have the power to know. To know what? To know the essence of Christ, the extent of his love. Yet that love is beyond knowledge. We can't imagine how wide and long and high and deep it is. But as our knowledge of God and Christ grows, we grasp more of the love that they are. That love fills us and spills from us to all we meet.

Do you want to know God? Then pray. Ask to know him. Do you sometimes feel hopeless? Then pray. Ask to know the sure hope he calls us to. Are you sometimes powerless against the forces arrayed against you? Pray for power. Power to overcome. Power to know the love of Christ. Do not face your problems on your own. Power is yours. All you have to do is ask.

Questions for further discussion

1. Do you often pray for other Christians to be encouraged? Do you ask them to pray for your own encouragement? Isn't this as legitimate a prayer request as praying for the sick?

2. Should we pray for weak Christians? What should our prayer be for them? Is there a temptation to feel superior to them?

3. Think of some situations when you needed comfort from God and other Christians. Have you prayed lately for others in a similar situation? What is the best way we can comfort others?

4. Can Christians be perfect? What do we mean by "perfect"? What does the Bible mean by it? Should we pray that others might be perfect?

5. How are prayer and Bible study related? How do we come to know God in prayer? What do we want to know about him? How does knowledge bring power?

CHAPTER EIGHT

WE HAVE NOT CEASED PRAYING FOR YOU: PAUL'S PRAYERS FOR THE CHURCHES (II)

What I'm about to say may shock you, especially those of you who have been in church all of your life. But it's the truth and I must say it.

I've never been part of a bad church. Every church I've experienced has been full of people who gave of themselves fully and freely, who showed love to the downtrodden, who expressed the true joy of God. Sure, there were rare church members who gossiped, lied, and cheated, but they were rare.

So how do you pray for a good church? What do you say about Christians whose lives seem much more exemplary than your own? Paul knew such a church, and he knew how to pray for them.

For the Philippians (Philippians 1:3-6, 9-11)

Every church has its problems and its strong points, but if one church in the New Testament is a model church, it is the church at Philippi. When Paul wrote the Philippians, the tone of his letter was completely positive with lavish praise for them. This tone was set in his prayer for them,

> I thank my God every time I remember you, constantly praying with joy in every one of my prayers for all of you, because of your sharing in the gospel from the first day until now. I am confident of this, that the one who began a good work

among you will bring it to completion by the day of Jesus Christ . . .. And this is my prayer, that your love may overflow more and more with knowledge and full insight to help you determine what is best, so that in the day of Christ you may be pure and blameless, having produced the harvest of righteousness that comes through Jesus Christ for the glory and praise of God (1:3-6, 9-11).

Paul's prayers for the Philippians were prayers of joy. Joy and rejoicing are central themes in this letter. Paul introduced these themes in his prayer. What was it about the Philippians that made Paul rejoice? Their sharing in the gospel. The Philippians had gladly received the gospel as the saving truth from God. More than that, they had supported Paul's proclamation of the gospel through their generous gifts and their prayers. Yet this good work was not their own doing, Paul said. Christ had begun it, and Paul prayed that he would bring it to completion at the last day.

Paul's prayer for the Philippians is quite similar to his prayer for the Corinthians and the Ephesians. As with the Ephesians, he wants God to grant them love and knowledge. Paul wants the Ephesians to know the love of God; he wants the Philippians' love to overflow with knowledge. In Christianity, love and knowledge go hand in hand. To know God is to love him. If we love him, we come to know him more.

This knowledge of God is more than simply an intellectual achievement. Knowing God changes the way we think, the way we live, the way we treat others. As Paul prayed for the Corinthians, so he prays for the Philippians that the God they know and love will produce good lives, a "harvest of righteousness," that they may be pure and blameless on the day of Christ.

Is this the way we pray for our fellow Christians? It seems to me that most of our prayers are for the healing and comfort of people. Nothing is wrong with those prayers. Paul also prays for the healing and consolation of his brothers and sisters. But he is primarily concerned with their standing before God. From Paul the church today can learn to pray for what is most important – that we and our fellow Christians may know the love of God and may live blameless lives, looking forward to that final endless day of Jesus Christ.

For the Colossians (Colossians 1:3-5, 9-12)

It is not surprising that Paul repeats himself in his prayers for the different churches. After all, most churches are similar, facing the same struggles and sharing the same joys. We must remember that these are not Paul's actual prayers, but his reports of his prayers. If we could hear Paul pray for the churches, we would no doubt find his prayers personalized to fit each congregation.

When we come to Paul's prayer for the Colossian church, we find little that is new. Colossians is written about the same time as Ephesians, and the two letters are quite similar. Paul's prayer for the Colossians thus echoes many themes of his other prayers.

> In our prayers for you we always thank God, the Father of our Lord Jesus Christ, for we have heard of your faith in Christ Jesus and of the love that you have for all the saints, because of the hope laid up for you in heaven.
>
> For this reason, since the day we heard it, we have not ceased praying for you and asking that you may be filled with the knowledge of God's will in all spiritual wisdom and understanding, so that you may lead lives worthy of the Lord, fully pleasing to him, as you bear fruit in every good work and as you grow in the knowledge of God. May you be strong with all the strength that comes from his glorious power, and may you be prepared to endure everything with patience, while joyfully giving thanks to the Father, who has enabled you to share in the inheritance of the saints in the light (1:3-5, 9-12).

Here we encounter Paul's usual prayer vocabulary. He thanks God for their faith, hope, and love, and prays for them to receive the knowledge that brings good works, strength, and endurance. The new themes he emphasizes in Colossians are hope and endurance, perhaps reflecting the sufferings of the church or of Paul himself, since he writes this from prison (4:10). In either case, he speaks of the need for endurance. The power to endure springs from a great doctrine of Christianity – the hope laid up for us in heaven.

The Bible's definition of hope is the opposite of the way we usually use the word. In everyday use, to hope is to wish fondly for something – "I hope it doesn't rain today," "I hope the boss gives me a raise," "I hope little Johnny is all right" – wishes with varying degrees of certainty about their outcome. In the Scriptures hope is a sure thing, because it is based not on our own actions, but on the gracious act of God in Jesus Christ.

Growing up as a Christian, I remember several occasions when older Christians were asked, "If you died today, would you go to heaven?" Almost invariably they answered, "I hope so," in much the same tone they used to say, "I hope it doesn't rain today." The one exception was an elderly woman in our church who promptly replied, "Yes, I know I'd go to heaven." When asked how she could be so sure, she said simply, "God told me I was saved and I believe him." This lady knew the true meaning of Christian hope. Did not Christ say, "I go to prepare a place for you?" Didn't he pray that we should share his glory? If we believe him, our hope is sure.

But the hope of heaven is much more than pie in the sky when you die by and by. Our hope awaits us in heaven, but it also guides our present lives. Some people are afraid that assurance of salvation and certainty of hope will lead Christians to neglect their Christian duties. If we already have it made, why work for it? Paul sees hope in a different light. He thanks God for the Colossians' hope because it motivates their faith in Christ and their love for the saints. Hope in their inheritance gives them power to endure. Certainty of hope moves Christians to loving action for God and neighbor.

What has all of this to do with prayer? We, too, should thank God for the hope within us and for the hope we see in fellow Christians. What is more, hope forms the context for every prayer we pray. We could not pray without hope of being heard. We could not pray, "Your will be done," if we had no sure hope that God's will would ultimately triumph. His will is for us to be saved. We always pray with confidence. We always pray in hope.

For the Thessalonians (1 Thessalonians 1:2-3; 3:9-13; 2 Thessalonians 1:3, 11-12)

The Thessalonian letters are probably the earliest letters of Paul, but they already contain his distinctive prayer vocabulary: *"We always give thanks to God for all of you and mention you in our prayers, constantly remembering before our God and Father your work of faith and labor of love and steadfastness of hope in our Lord Jesus Christ"* (1 Thessalonians 1:2-3).

Faith, hope, love. Paul's three favorite words. This is what he thanks God for. But these are more than theological terms for Paul, more than just church words for use on Sunday. They are action words. He thanks God for their work of faith. True faith always shows itself in action, in work for God and neighbor. Paul thanks God for their labor of love. Love is no good if it is love in name only. Love must express itself in work for others. Paul thanks God for their steadfastness of hope. Here is no mere wishing thinking, but a sure hope that inspires endurance. To Paul, faith, hope, and love are not simply theological virtues. They always lead to ethical action. They are gifts from God and causes for thanksgiving.

Later in 1 Thessalonians we have an account of Paul's prayers for them and one of those prayers:

> How can we thank God enough for you in return for all the joy that we feel before our God because of you? Night and day we pray most earnestly that we may see you face to face and restore whatever is lacking in your faith.
>
> Now may our God and Father himself and our Lord Jesus direct our way to you. And may the Lord make you increase and abound in love for one another and for all, just as we abound in love for you. And may he so strengthen your hearts in holiness that you may be blameless before our God and Father at the coming of our Lord Jesus with all his saints (3:9-13).

Paul is so overwhelmed with the joy he feels when he thinks of the believers in Thessalonica that he breaks out in blessing. Thankful to God for that joy, he asks God to increase their love and to make them holy and blameless.

How often do we pray for holiness today? "Holiness" carries overtones of hypocrisy or fanaticism, but it is an essential biblical word that we should work to recover. To be genuinely holy is not to be "holier than thou." Instead, it is transformation into the image of Christ. Holiness is not an option for Christians. We must be holy to stand blameless before God at the coming of Jesus. But holiness is not the result of our own spiritual fervor or discipline. It is a gift of God, a gift sought in prayer. It is God who sanctifies us, who disciplines us, who presents us blameless. As Paul prayed for the Thessalonian Christians, so we should pray for God to strengthen our hearts in holiness.

Paul repeats his thanksgiving and requests for the church in 2 Thessalonians:

> We must always give thanks to God for you, brothers and sisters, as is right, because your faith is growing abundantly, and the love of everyone of you for one another is increasing.
>
> To this end we always pray for you, asking that our God will make you worthy of his call and will fulfill by his power every good resolve and work of faith, so that the name of our Lord Jesus may be glorified in you, and you in him, according to the grace of our God and the Lord Jesus Christ (1:3, 11-12).

Again Paul is thankful for their faith and prays God to empower their work of faith. He also prays God will make them worthy of his call. Here is a look backward and a look forward. We Christians look back to the moment God called us from a life of sin and we obeyed that call (2 Thessalonians 2:13-14). At that moment no one was worthy. All of us were sinners without hope. Still God called us to eternal life. Thus we look forward to the coming of our Lord (2 Thessalonians 1:10). Between the time of our calling and the time of our glory, God works in us to make us worthy of his call. For that we pray.

For Timothy (2 Timothy 1:3-5)

Gratitude for his fellow Christians marks Paul's life, and he is especially thankful for Timothy, his son in the faith. Paul calls him "my beloved child" and says:

> I am grateful to God – whom I worship with a clear conscience, as my ancestors did – when I remember you constantly in my prayers night and day. Recalling your tears, I long to see you so that I may be filled with joy. I am reminded of your sincere faith, a faith that lived first in your grandmother Lois and your mother Eunice and now, I am sure, lives in you (2 Timothy 1:3-5).

Since Timothy's father was Greek (and by implication an unbeliever), Paul became Timothy's surrogate father. Timothy is blessed by two strong women in his life, Lois and Eunice, who taught him to have faith in God. Paul is thankful for these women, and thankful for Timothy's love for them and him. Timothy's tears stand as a witness of his love for Paul.

"Faith of our fathers, holy faith," we sometimes sing. But what about the faith of our mothers? For Timothy and for many of us, it was a faithful mother or grandmother who first taught us of Jesus. Some of my earliest memories are of Mom tucking me into bed and reading me a Bible story. Few of us come to faith on our own; our families nurture our faith, sometimes through great effort and sacrifice.

We, too, have the duty and the honor of ensuring our children will have faith. To possess a faithful mother, grandmother, father, brother, sister, and child is a great boon from God. In prayer we, like Paul, thank him for those whose lives bless ours.

For Philemon (Philemon 1:4-7)

This faith we have from our families is not a precious commodity to hoard. It is a precious commodity to share. Paul writes Philemon and rejoices that he shares his faith with others.

> When I remember you in my prayers, I always thank my God

> because I hear of your love for all the saints and your faith toward the Lord Jesus. I pray that the sharing of your faith may become effective when you perceive all the good that we do for Christ. I have indeed received much joy and encouragement from your love, because the hearts of the saints have been refreshed through you, my brother (Philemon 1:4-7).

Sharing our faith usually means evangelism, and that is probably what Paul has in mind here. However, we also share our faith with fellow Christians, refreshing their hearts. To share faith also means to do good for Christ. In Philemon's case, doing good meant receiving and forgiving Onesimus, his runaway slave.

Share the faith. This brief phrase summarizes the whole of the Christian life. If our faith is genuine, we will tell others the good news of Jesus. Our faith will encourage the hearts of the faithful. Our faith will lead us to good works, even to accept and forgive those who have wronged us. We thank God for our faith and the faith of others, and we pray for courage to share that faith.

Praying with Paul

What can we learn from Paul's prayers for the churches? First, we see Paul constantly in prayer. Like Jesus, he had a habit of prayer. We also must make prayer a regular part of our lives. Prayer is not just for church time, for meals, or at bedtime. These are appropriate times for prayer, but they must not exhaust our prayer life. Prayer is for all times and any time.

Paul prayed for others. The biblical word for this is intercession, a word we do not often use. But we must follow the practice. Other Christians desperately need our prayers, and we need theirs. Paul realized he needed the prayers of the churches, so he often asked for their prayers. We must not be too proud to ask our brothers and sisters to pray for us. We also must not be so wrapped up in our own concerns that we forget the needs of others. In Christ, we are all in this thing together. We need help. We need to pray.

We should also note that Paul's requests to God for the

churches and the causes of his thankfulness to God, were usually spiritual matters. He rarely thanked God for their health or wealth, but he was thankful for their faith, hope, and love. He seldom asked God to bless them with the ordinary blessings of life, but he did beseech God to give them spiritual discernment, steadfastness, and power. It is not wrong to ask for health or daily bread, but Paul knew what was really of value. When we pray for others or for ourselves, we must also ask God for the big blessings, the spiritual gifts, for only they will last into the coming kingdom.

Finally, it seems significant that Paul told his readers he prayed for them. In those rough weeks when everything goes wrong, when there are tests of faith and we hover on the edge of despair, how marvelous it is to hear someone say, "I am praying for you." We should not only pray for our brothers and sisters in Christ, we should encourage them by telling them how thankful we are to God for them and how we have asked his blessing to be on them.

Questions for further discussion

1. What gives you joy in prayer? Do our prayers become less joyful when we pray for those in need? What can we do to rejoice more in prayer?

2. Do you often thank God for the faith of other Christians? Do you thank him for hope? How can we focus more in prayer on what God has done for us spiritually?

3. What is holiness? How does God make us holy? What part does prayer play?

4. How often have you resolved to do something good and then neglected to do it? How often have you heard prayers that God would strengthen our resolve?

5. What keeps us from sharing our faith with others? What should we pray concerning this?

CHAPTER NINE

GIVE THANKS IN ALL CIRCUMSTANCES: PAUL'S TEACHING ON PRAYER

As we have seen, Paul is a man of prayer. He prays for the churches but he also gives them instructions on how to pray. Like most Christians today, his readers probably associate the word "prayer" with making a request from God. Asking God for what we need is part of prayer, but it does not exhaust its meaning.

Giving Thanks (2 Corinthians 8:16; Ephesians 5:19-20; Colossians 3:15-16; 1 Thessalonians 5:16-18; 1 Timothy 1:12-14)

Paul frequently reminds his readers that thanksgiving is also a necessary part of prayer. Praising and thanking God for his marvelous gifts is prayer's true essence. Sometimes Paul models this spirit of thanksgiving by breaking out in prayer in the middle of his letters. For example, in the middle of a discussion of the contribution for the poor Christians in Judea he says, *"But thanks be to God who put in the heart of Titus the same eagerness for you that I myself had"* (2 Corinthians 8:16). Titus' concern for the Corinthians does not spring from himself. It is the gift of God. To Paul any attitude that promotes the spread of the gospel and leads to unity among Christians is a gift of God. Today we need the same faith to see spiritual growth in the church as God gift to us instead of something we do for him. Like Paul, we should be thankful for that gift.

At times our hearts are so full of the joy of thanksgiving

that we cannot express it in mere words. At those times, only song can truly express our gratitude.

> Let the peace of Christ rule in your hearts, to which indeed you were called in one body. And be thankful. Let the word of Christ dwell in you richly; teach and admonish one another in all wisdom; and with gratitude in your hearts sing psalms, hymns, and spiritual songs to God. And whatever you do, in word or deed, do everything in the name of the Lord Jesus, giving thanks to God the Father through him
> (Colossians 3:15-17; see also Ephesians 5:18-20).

Singing does many things for the Christian. Christ's word dwells within us as we sing. We teach and encourage one another in song. What is more important, we praise our holy God in song, singing with gratitude in our hearts for all he has done for us. These songs of thanksgiving are also prayers to him.

But what if we don't feel like singing? What if we've had a terrible day? What if we can't find anything to be thankful for? The Bible says for us to sing anyway. Pray even when you don't feel like it. Be thankful even in trouble, as Paul says, "giving thanks to God the Father at all times and for everything in the name of our Lord Jesus Christ" (Ephesians 5:20).

How can we be thankful always? How can we sing with gratitude when we don't feel it? Is Paul demanding the impossible or is he advocating hypocrisy? Does he want us to fake our gratitude when we are not in the mood to be genuinely grateful?

None of the above. Paul simply realizes that thankfulness is not an emotion but an attitude. Paul himself does not always feel like thanking God. Stoned, shipwrecked, beaten, imprisoned, and even given a thorn in the flesh, he knows the meaning of suffering and pain, yet he can give thanks always and for everything. How? Because he trusts God to bring good out of evil, blessing out of suffering. He knows his current pains cannot be compared with the glory he will receive. That's how he and Silas can sing praises from a prison cell (Acts 16:25).

So are we to thank God for the trouble that comes upon us? Can we honestly thank God for broken bones, for terminal diseases, for the loss of our loved ones? No. We must remember our loving Father does not send evil. Paul's thorn in the flesh was from Satan, not from God (2 Corinthians 12:9). God did not remove the thorn, but he used that evil as an occasion to give grace, "My grace is sufficient for you." We are not thankful for trouble, but we can thank God for everything that happens to us if we trust him to suffer with us and to turn our pain to glory. And that is precisely what he has promised.

Thus Paul can say, *"Rejoice always, pray without ceasing, give thanks in all circumstances; for this is the will of God in Christ Jesus for you"* (1Thessalonians 5:16-18). God's will is for us to give thanks in all circumstances. No matter what horrors face us in life, we can always identify something to be thankful for, so we can pray without ceasing. When suffering, don't stop praying, but find some way to be thankful to God.

Our salvation is one thing we can always thank God for. When trouble comes, we know God still loves us because he sent his Son to save us. Paul reflects this awareness when he prays,

> I am grateful to Jesus Christ our Lord, who has strengthened me, because he judged me faithful and appointed me to his service, even though I was formerly a blasphemer, a persecutor, and a man of violence. But I received mercy because I had acted ignorantly in unbelief, and the grace of our Lord overflowed for me with the faith and love that are in Christ Jesus. The saying is sure and worthy of full acceptance, that Jesus Christ came into the world to save sinners – of whom I am foremost (1 Timothy 1:12-15).

Paul can stand any hardship because God saved him, the foremost of sinners, saved him when he was on the road to Damascus to kill more Christians. Paul never forgets he was a sinner, nor does he forget the ongoing grace of God. So he can be grateful to God no matter what comes his way.

Today trouble comes to us and threatens to overwhelm.

We cry in pain wondering how a loving God could allow this to happen to his children, but we must not doubt his love. If he did not spare his own Son for us, will he not give us all we need? Surely he will. And for that we are always thankful.

Public Prayer (1 Corinthians 11:2-13; 14:13-19; 1 Timothy 2:1-8)

There are times for us to pray alone, times for us to pray with a few fellow Christians, but also times when the whole church prays together. These public prayers take place as we worship each Sunday and at other times when churches assemble. Christian assemblies in the first century were quite different from ours in some ways, but they always included corporate prayer to God. The Corinthian church has severe problems in their worship –drunkenness at the Lord's Supper, divisions in the assembly, confusion when several spoke in tongues or prophesied at once – so Paul writes them concerning propriety in worship and public prayer:

> Any man who prays or prophesies with something on his head disgraces his head, but any woman who prays or prophesies with her head unveiled disgraces her head– it is one and the same thing as having her head shaved.
>
> Judge for yourselves: is it proper for a woman to pray to God with her head unveiled? Does not nature itself teach you that if a man wears long hair, it is degrading to him, but if a woman has long hair, it is her glory? For her hair is given to her for a covering. But if anyone is disposed to be contentious – we have no such custom, nor do the churches of God (1 Corinthians 11:4-5, 13-16).

In this lengthy passage, Paul speaks of a custom familiar to his readers but foreign to our society, the wearing of veils. He also speaks about a hot topic in the contemporary church, the role of women in worship and church leadership. These are interesting and important topics, but our question now is what this passage has to say to the modern church concerning prayer.

If we avoid Paul's difficult arguments on veils, authority,

and angels, one teaching about public prayer comes through clearly. He assumes that both men and women will pray when the church comes together. Does this mean women lead prayer? I'm not sure. "Leading in prayer" is modern church practice. In Corinth, it appears that different individuals pray aloud in the assembly when moved by the Holy Spirit. Thus, a man or a woman may pray aloud. Paul is not attempting to keep women from praying, but he does want to make sure that both women and men wear acceptable cultural dress as they pray.

Women like men need to pray in church. Of course, when someone leads in prayer, all Christians in the assembly, whether male or female, pray with the leader. Paul may be saying more than this. There are times when Christians should raise their voices to God in prayer, one at a time, and some of those voices might be feminine. Our churches might be stronger if we heard our brothers and sisters pray aloud. This does not mean all distinctions between men and women disappear in church, for the primary purpose of this passage is to dispel that notion. But we must remember that women, no less than men, are heirs of salvation and have a Father who hears their prayers.

Paul's second concern with public prayer in Corinth is that it is understandable. Several Corinthians can speak in tongues, they can pray in what some consider to be a special prayer language. Such prayer is helpful in private, but in public assemblies of the church it does not build up other Christians and it confuses the outsider:

> If I pray in a tongue, my spirit prays but my mind is unproductive. What should I do then? I will pray with the spirit, but I will pray with the mind also; I will sing praise with the spirit, but I will sing praise with the mind also. Otherwise, if you say a blessing with the spirit, how can anyone in the position of an outsider say the "Amen" to your thanksgiving, since the outsider does not know what you are saying? For you may give thanks well enough, but the other person is not built up. I thank God that I speak in tongues more than all of you; nevertheless, in church I would rather speak five words with

> my mind, in order to instruct others also, than ten thousand words in a tongue (1 Corinthians 14:14-19).

Tongue speaking is another controversial topic among contemporary Christians. Some claim to speak in tongues, others dispute that claim. This passage clearly says that even if one can speak in tongues, the gift has no place in public prayer. Christians must understand prayers they pray together. All must say "Amen" to the prayer.

But what if we cannot speak in tongues or do not even believe the gift is available today? Does this passage have a message for those who are noncharismatic? Yes. The principle of understandable public prayer applies to all churches. Tongues are not the only obstacle to understanding prayer. Such things as mumbling, using an unfamiliar vocabulary, slipping into a strange "prayer tone," and praying only for our personal situation can make for obscure public prayers. We must be clear when we pray in church. We must realize that others pray with us. We must even consider the outsiders who come to our assembly. Our worship should not confuse or offend them. If they are offended, it must be by the offense of the gospel and not by our unintelligible prayers.

Public prayer should focus in two directions simultaneously. We can never forget that we pray to God. He is the only one to whom we speak in prayer. Meanwhile we must be aware of our fellow Christians, for we pray together. It is our joint prayers that ascend to the Father. Public prayer must speak only to God, but it must also build up our brothers and sisters.

What kind of prayers should we offer in public? Who should we pray for? How should we pray? Paul tackles these questions in 1 Timothy.

> First of all, then, I urge that supplications, prayers, intercessions, and thanksgivings be made for everyone, for kings and all who are in high positions so that we may lead a quiet and peaceable life in all godliness and dignity. . . I desire, then, that in every place the men should pray, lifting up holy hands without anger or argument (2:1-2, 8).

Four words here describe prayer.

- *Supplications*are heartfelt requests to God for help

through personal difficulty.

• *Prayers* also implies requests from God, but in a broader sense of asking for his care in all circumstances.

• *Intercessions* are prayers for those around us. We petition God on behalf of our brothers, sisters, and neighbors.

• *Thanksgivings* spring naturally from our gratitude for God's gifts.

These terms do not describe four separate types of prayer, but point to elements found in most public prayers. In church we make requests to God for ourselves and for others, and we thank him for his blessings.

We pray these prayers for everyone, but particularly for kings and those in high position. In Paul's day many rulers persecute Christians, yet believers are to pray even for unjust rulers in hope that God will make the bad kings leave Christians in peace. Our God is so powerful he can work through evil rulers to accomplish his purposes. No matter what kind of government rules us, we still pray the authorities will allow us to live quiet and peaceable Christian lives.

On the subject of *how* to pray, we are to lift up holy hands. This raises the subject of bodily posture in prayer. The Bible gives many positions for prayer: standing, kneeling, bowing the face to the ground, lifting hands, and others. No single position is promoted as the only proper way of praying. In public or private prayer we may kneel or bow or stand or raise hands. What we may not do is belittle a brother or sister who prays in a different posture. Prayer must be without anger or argument. Neither should we adopt an unusual prayer position to call attention to ourselves and our hyper-spirituality. Our church's custom should dictate our practice. Public prayer is a time for Christians to be united in their petitions to God. It is not a time (there is never an acceptable time) for us to bicker and argue over how we pray. Attitude, not posture, decides the genuineness of our prayers.

Having said this, it does appear to me that our posture says something about our attitude in prayer. In Old Testament times it was common to throw oneself face downward in prayer to express respect for the Almighty. In my own boyhood I remember how sincerely impressed I was to see men and women kneeling in prayer. We can make too much of "body language," but I wonder why we stopped kneeling. Was it the inconvenience or a lack of reverence?

Whatever our posture, something special happens when the church prays together. The routine of our worship services may blind us to the beauty of corporate prayer. In a world where everyone looks out for number one, Christians put aside their differences and join to approach their Father and encourage each other. What could be more beautiful?

Questions for further discussion

1. Doesn't something special happen when we sing prayers? What are some of your favorite prayer hymns? Why do sung prayers sometimes seem more meaningful than spoken prayers?
2. Did women pray with men in Corinth? Do you think the women prayed aloud? Does this happen today? Should it?
3. What are some ways we can pray together without only one person leading? Should we pray more often in these ways?
4. Discuss the difference between supplications, prayers, intercession, and thanksgiving. Should all our prayers include these?
5. Does posture in prayer make a difference? Why do we fail to use some biblical postures?

CHAPTER TEN

PRAY IN THE SPIRIT AT ALL TIMES: PAUL'S TEACHING ON PRAYER (II)

In his letters Paul gives thanks for the churches and prays that God will grant them certain spiritual blessings. He does not, however, think himself spiritually superior to his readers. He not only prays for them, he requests their prayers.

Requesting Prayer (Romans 15:30-33; 2 Corinthians 1:10-11; Philippians 1:19; Ephesians 6:18-20; Colossians 4:2-4; 1 Thessalonians 5:25; 2 Thessalonians 3:1-5)

Paul is not a spiritual loner. He knows his limitations and knows that many oppose the gospel. Thus, he frequently asks his fellow Christians to support him through prayer.

> I appeal to you, brothers and sisters, by our Lord Jesus Christ and by the love of the Spirit, to join me in earnest prayer to God on my behalf, that I may be rescued from the unbelievers in Judea, and that my ministry to Jerusalem may be acceptable to the saints, so that by God's will I may come to you with joy and be refreshed in your company. The God of peace be with all of you. Amen (Romans 15:30-33).

Two nagging concerns overshadow Paul's coming trip to Jerusalem. One is the opposition he will face there. This is no figment of Paul's imagination. Already the unbelieving Jews have tried to kill him (Acts 9:29-30). Their hatred of Paul is understandable. To them he is a turncoat, one who once stood firm for the Law and against these wayward Jews who are loyal to the Nazarene, but now has himself been deceived into following Jesus. Paul knows their hatred and their power, so he asks the Romans to pray for his deliverance that he may afterward come to visit them in Rome (Romans 15:32; see also Philemon 1:22). Their prayer for Paul is answered, though not in the way Paul expected. He is delivered from death in Jerusalem, but he comes to Rome in chains, a prisoner because of the unbelievers (Acts 21:27-28:31).

This is not the only time when Paul faces danger from unbelievers. Everywhere he goes, he makes enemies. In Asia, he faces a severe trial that threatens to completely crush his spirit (2 Corinthians 1:8-11). But God rescues him then, and he is confident God will save him again. Paul has this confidence through prayer. He asks the Corinthians and the Romans to "join us by helping us by your prayers" (2 Corinthians 1:11; see also Philippians 1:19; 2 Thessalonians 3:1-2). Paul never faces opposition alone. Through prayer his fellow Christians and his heavenly Father stand beside him.

Paul's second concern regarding his Judean trip seems less realistic to us, but he knows the temper of the Jerusalem church better than we can. He worries that his ministry to the Jerusalem church (the gift of money he collected from the Gentile churches) will be rejected. Why would the Jerusalem Christian reject a gift for the poor, a gift they themselves have asked Paul to remember (see Acts 11:27-30; Galatians 2:10)? Because this was no ordinary gift. It was a gift from predominantly Gentile churches to the Jewish church in Jerusalem. Paul hopes this gift will cement relations between Jews and Gentiles in the church since it proves the love of Gentile Christians for their Jewish brothers and sisters. By receiving the gift, the Jerusalem church will be admitting that Gentiles are fully heirs of Christ along with the Jews.

Don't forget that the Judaizers dog Paul's every step during this stage in his ministry. They refuse to admit Gentiles into the church unless they first become Jews. These Judaizers are influential in the Jerusalem church and it would not be out of character for them to let people starve rather than compromise their principles to receive a gift from Gentiles. So Paul is requesting the Romans to pray for unity among Christians. Their prayer is answered. The Jerusalem church welcomes Paul and accepts his gift warmly (Acts 21:17-20).

What do these requests for prayer say to Christians today? We also face opposition from unbelievers. They may not try to kill us, but they can insult and wound. God will deliver us from such people if we pray. We also face disunity and bad feelings between Christians. We must join to pray for unity so that the good gifts we have for one another are graciously accepted.

When ridiculed for our Christian faith, our first reaction is to keep a low profile, to soft-peddle our Christianity, or to keep completely quiet about it. Paul faces more than ridicule; he faces imprisonment, beatings, and death. He would be less than human if he is not at times tempted to be quiet about Christ. Facing that temptation, he asks the churches to pray for him:

> Pray also for me, so that when I speak, a message may be given to me to make known with boldness the mystery of the gospel, for which I am an ambassador in chains. Pray that I might declare it boldly, as I must speak (Ephesians 6:19-20).

> Devote yourselves to prayer, keeping alert in it with thanksgiving. At the same time pray for us as well that God will open a door for the word, that we may declare the mystery of Christ, for which I am in prison, so that I may reveal it clearly, as I should (Colossians 4:2-4).

In these passages Paul asks for boldness to proclaim the mystery of the gospel. He knows opposition can make his witness timid. He knows how easy it is to soften the offensive teachings of the Christian message, so he prays that he may reveal Christ clearly.

The puny opposition we face from a hostile culture tempts us also to weaken our witness. We say, "Yes, I'm a

Christian, but I don't condemn those who aren't," or "I believe the Bible, but if you don't, you're entitled to your opinion," or "I don't want to force my beliefs on anyone." Or we say nothing at all. We are completely silent about our faith in the presence of unbelievers. But if Jesus is who he says he is, and if we take our faith seriously, then we must tell the Good News. If Christianity is true, it should be "forced" on people – that is, we must make them admit it's truth. Christian witness is not optional. We either confess Christ or we don't. If we fail to confess him, he will fail to confess us.

But where can we get the courage to confess Christ when it is embarrassing and may even cost us friendships, promotions, and acceptance? Only in prayer. If the bold apostle Paul needs to ask for courage and boldness, surely we need to ask. And we should pray for God to make other Christians bold.

Christians are not to live their Christian lives alone. Our prayer lives are not to be merely private. Like Paul we need at times to say, "Beloved, pray for us (1 Thessalonians 5:25). It is only through the prayers of our brothers and sisters and the blessing of our heavenly Father that we can live the demanding life of a bold Christian.

Prayer, Anxiety, and Suffering (Romans 12:12; 2 Corinthians 12:7-10; Philippians 4:6-7)

Jesus had a habit of private prayeı. The early Jerusalem church devoted themselves to prayer. Paul tells the Thessalonians to "pray without ceasing" (1 Thessalonians 5:17). As Christians we must develop a consistent prayer life in all circumstances. However, times will come that particularly call for prayer. Jesus prays in the crises of his life. The early Christians pray at the turning points in the life of the church. We, too, should pray in the face of suffering and anxiety.

Paul tells the Romans, *"Rejoice in hope, be patient in suffering, persevere in prayer"* (Romans 12:12). We must be persistent in prayer even in our darkest hours. The pressures of life sometimes threaten to overwhelm us. In our despair there is the temptation to stop praying, thinking, "What's the use?"

But perseverance in prayer leads to patience in suffering, and no matter how bad things get, we can still rejoice in the hope of resurrection. Our suffering may even be fatal, but it is not final. God holds us in his hand.

These two strange bedfellows – rejoicing and suffering – are found together in other New Testament passages. Paul urges the Philippians to rejoice and be thankful even in the midst of anxiety:

> Rejoice in the Lord always; again I will say, Rejoice. Let your gentleness be known to everyone. The Lord is near. Do not worry about anything, but in everything by prayer and supplication with thanksgiving let your requests be made known to God. And the peace of God, which passes all understanding, will guard your hearts and your minds in Christ Jesus (4:4-7).

This is a reassuring Scripture. Christian joy stems not from circumstances, but from the realization that "the Lord is near." The lives we live may produce great anxiety, but if we take thankfully that worry to God, he will give us peace that passes understanding.

The sure solution to worry promised by these verses is quite different from the prescriptions of our age. Paul does not urge us to think positively, to believe in ourselves, or to minimize the reasons for our worry. Dedicated Christians have good reasons for worry. After all, the world is against us. Our promised peace is not the result of a twelve-step program or any particular technique. It is the free gift of God in prayer. It is a peace that passes understanding because it is based not on the pleasantness of our circumstances, but on our trust in a Father who guards us.

It is also strange peace because even when we persist in prayer, God does not always relieve the cause of our anxiety. Paul knows this personally. When he speaks of pain and anxiety, he speaks not as a bystander, but as one who knows such feelings intimately.

> Therefore to keep me from being too elated, a thorn was given me in the flesh, a messenger of Satan to torment me, to keep me from being too elated. Three times I appealed to the

> Lord about this, that it would leave me, but he said to me, "My grace is sufficient for you, for power is made perfect in weakness." So, I will boast all the more gladly of my weaknesses, so that the power of Christ may dwell in me. Therefore I am content with weaknesses, insults, hardships, persecutions, and calamities for the sake of Christ; for whenever I am weak, then I am strong (2 Corinthians 12:7-10).

Speculation on the exact nature of Paul's thorn in the flesh is fruitless. Whatever it was, it caused him pain and anxiety. He does not blame God for the thorn. It is "a messenger of Satan," he says, but he does make his request for relief to God. God's answer: "My grace is sufficient for you."

What kind of answer is this? Has God not promised to heal our hurts and remove our worries? Yes. And that is precisely what he does for Paul. He does not remove the pain, but he makes it of no account. He places it in a new perspective. "My grace is enough," God says, "for my power is made perfect in weakness." The loving Father offers Paul more than healing. He offers grace and perfection. God did not send the thorn, but he is so powerful he can take this evil thing and use it for Paul's good. Paul is not healed, but God takes away his anxiety as grace swallos his pain.

God's answer to Paul, and the three prayers Paul offers, remind us of another sufferer who cried to God in pain. Like Jesus in Gethsemane, Paul has a cross to bear. Like Jesus, he trusts the will of the Father.

Jesus and Paul are not alone. Each Christian must take up the cross. Our call is to suffer with Jesus. God promises us relief from pain and anxiety, but he does not promise us cure for all our sicknesses or smooth paths to travel. In pain we cry to God, and he hears us. He may remove the pain, or he may say, "My grace is enough. You must bear this cross." That answer should be enough for us, for he suffers with us, perfecting us in weakness and giving us a sure hope.

The Help of the Spirit (Romans 8:26-28; Ephesians 6:18)

All this sounds marvelous, but can we really do it? Can we really pray that God's will be done? Can we be happy with

God's answer if he chooses not to heal our pain? What should we pray for? Healing? Faith? Courage? Resignation? How do we know what God's will is for us?

These questions point to one fact –when it comes to prayer, we need help. The good news is that we have it.

> Likewise the Spirit helps us in our weakness; for we do not know how to pray as we ought, but that very Spirit intercedes with sighs too deep for words. And God, who searches the heart, knows what is the mind of the Spirit, because the Spirit intercedes for the saints according to the will of God (Romans 8:26-27).

"We do not know how to pray as we ought." Were truer words ever spoken? Like the disciples, we must ask, "Lord, teach us to pray." But this passage deals less with the technique of prayer than with the content of prayer. Not only do we not know the right words to say, we do not even know what to pray for. All of us have had loved ones on the verge of death. At such a time, what should we pray for? For healing? Perhaps, for even if the doctors have given up hope, our God still has life in his hands. But what if it is not God's will to heal this time? Do we pray for our loved one to face death with courage? Do we pray for a quick and painless death?

These are not hypothetical questions. Most of us have struggled with these situations. But we do not pray alone, for the Spirit prays with us. He takes our stumbling words, our doubts, and our struggles, and he translates them into "sighs too deep for words." We don't always know how to speak to God, but the Spirit knows, and he speaks for us. The effectiveness of prayer depends not on our ability to speak or on the clarity of our desires, but on the power of the Spirit.

Praying in the Spirit is the rule, not the exception in the Christian's prayer life. Truly spiritual prayer does not measure itself by how we feel, or how right we get the words. We don't have to pray "good" to pray in the Spirit. Even when we have no idea what to pray, even when we don't want to pray, the Spirit is there to help us. Yes, particularly when we can't pray, when we are victims of our weakness, the

Spirit intercedes. He amplifies our groanings as God's own megaphone, and God hears our cry.

So what should keep us from praying? Trouble? No, we are to take our worries to God. Our sins? No, for we rely on God's grace in prayer. Our own ineptitude? No, for the Spirit speaks for us. If we "pray in the Spirit at all times" (Ephesians 6:18), then our prayers are always adequate, even when we are not. We have no excuse, not even ourselves, for neglecting to pray.

Questions for further discussion

1. Are you ever in danger from unbelievers? Do we need to pray for boldness to speak God's word? What keeps us from speaking it?

2. Does prayer solve worry? How? Why don't we pray more and worry less?

3. Like Paul, have you ever prayed hard to have a problem removed and God did not remove it? Did that make you less likely to pray? Should it?

4. How does the Spirit help us when we pray? Do you think about and ask for the Spirit's help?

5. What keeps us from praying more?

CHAPTER ELEVEN

ASK IN FAITH, NEVER DOUBTING: PRAYER IN HEBREWS AND JAMES

The Gospels, Acts, and the Pauline writings are not the only New Testament books to mention prayer. Almost every New Testament book discusses prayer, showing how central prayer is to the life of Christ's disciples.

Prayer in Hebrews (Hebrews 5:7-10; 7:23-25; 13:18-19)

Hebrews is an unusual book. We are not sure who wrote it or who originally received it. It does not read like a letter or a history or a Gospel. Most scholars now believe Hebrews is a written sermon, since the author himself calls it a "brief word of exhortation" (13:22). To contemporary Christians it must seem like a strange sermon. It is not brief, at least not by our modern standards. It contains detailed arguments and obscure terminology from Old Testament sacrificial passages that modern audiences find difficult, if not downright impossible to follow.

In spite of its strangeness to the modern mind, Hebrews is a book to treasure by contemporary Christians. The writer of Hebrews displays the superiority and finality of Jesus, and he urges his readers to be faithful to the Pioneer of their salvation. In his reflection on the superiority of Jesus' high priesthood, he harks back to our Lord's prayers in Gethsemane: *"In the days of his flesh, Jesus offered up prayers and supplications, with loud cries and tears, to the one who was able to save him from death, and he was heard because of his reverent submission"* (Hebrews 5:7). In Gethsemane "with loud cries and tears,"

Jesus begged the Father to save him from death. Yet he prayed, "Your will be done."

When we read the Gospel accounts of Jesus in Gethsemane, it may seem that God did not hear Jesus' prayer. After all, Jesus did not receive what he asked for. He still had to go to the cross. According to the writer of Hebrews, however, God heard Jesus' prayer. In what sense did God *hear* his prayer? Does this simply mean that God heard him but said no to his request? I don't think so. To have one's prayer heard implies an answer, to receive God's blessing. The Hebrew writer contends God answered Jesus' prayer to be saved from death, but he did not answer in the way Jesus intended in his prayer. Christ still had to drink the cup, to go to the cross, but the Father saved him from death by raising him from the dead.

Perhaps, like me, you've heard that God answers prayer one of three ways: Yes, No, and Not Yet. This passage from Hebrews makes it clear that God has only one answer. If we ask in faith, and ask in the will of God as Jesus did in Gethsemane, then God always answers, "Yes." That "yes," however, may take a form better than expected: resurrection, new life, new self.

There is an important lesson for us here. God does not always give us what we want or what we think we need, but he always hears us and gives us something even better than we request. We may ask for relief from pain, for comfort for our broken hearts, for ease for our tired souls. He may not give us these. His answer may be, "My grace is sufficient for you," or "You must bear your cross," but he has a greater gift for us – the gift of resurrection, of new life. When we pray as Christians, we pray not with shallow optimism that things will immediately get better, but we pray with a sure hope that God will hear and bless in his own way and time. Like Jesus in Gethsemane, we may have to learn obedience through suffering (Hebrews 5:8-10), but like him we must maintain our faith in a loving Father who holds life in his hand, who answers our prayers.

By learning obedience, Jesus became our great high priest, the One who takes our sins to the Father.

> Furthermore, the former priests were many in number, because they were prevented by death from continuing in office; but he holds his priesthood permanently, because he continues forever. Consequently he is able for all time to save those who approach God through him, since he always lives to make intercession for them (7:23-25).

Jesus is our priest forever. He saves us for all time. Old Testament priests offered sacrifices repeatedly to cover the people's sins. Jesus offered himself for us once for all (Hebrews 7:27). As both our sacrifice and our priest, he lives to make intercession for us.

Why do we need intercession? Don't we have a heavenly Father who loves us and listens to us? Yes, but our sins have torn us away from the Father, blocking our path to the Most Holy God. But our Savior intercedes for us in prayer. He removes our sin, makes us right with God, and makes our requests for us. We can approach God boldly, for when we pray, Christ our priest and sacrifice prays with us. Our prayers become his prayers to the Father. He lives to pray for us.

The other reference to prayer in Hebrews sounds quite familiar: *"Pray for us; we are sure that we have a clear conscience, desiring to act honorably in all things. I urge you all the more to do this, so that I may be restored to you very soon"* (13:18-19).

As we saw with Paul, no Christian is so mature that he can afford to do without the prayers of other Christians. The Hebrew writer, like Paul, asks his readers to pray that he may see them soon, that he might "be restored to you." This is an intriguing phrase. Has there been bad blood between the writer and his readers? Is that why he insists he has a clear conscience? What has prevented him from going to them? Imprisonment? Sickness? Their own attitude? His work in other ministries? We are not told, but we do know he now wants to see them and he asks them to pray that he will.

Nothing should separate Christian brothers and sisters. Often we allow opinions or emotions to separate us. Perhaps someone said an inappropriate word, perhaps we felt ignored or ridiculed, perhaps neglect made us grow apart. From Hebrews we learn that the barriers existing between

Christians must be torn away by prayer. We must pray, and ask our fellow Christians to pray, that restoration will soon-take place between us.

Prayer in James

James' writing is full of practical advice for Christians, and so we would expect him to teach on prayer. At the very beginning of his book, after urging his readers to find joy even in trials, he tells them to ask for wisdom:

> If any of you is lacking in wisdom, ask God, who gives to all generously and ungrudgingly, and it will be given you. But ask in faith, never doubting, for the one who doubts is like a wave of the sea, driven and tossed by the wind; for the doubter, being double-minded and unstable in every way, must not expect to receive anything from the Lord (James 1:5-8).

Although the word "prayer" does not occur in this passage, we discover much of the importance on how to ask God for what we need. We are to ask for wisdom, something we need and God wants to give us. We especially need wisdom to see our daily trials as opportunities to strengthen our faith. We can pray in confidence, knowing that the God we pray to is generous and will give us the wisdom we need.

Yet this is no automatic transaction. James warns us to be careful how we ask. Our petitions to God must not be half-hearted. We cannot be undecided (in two minds) whether God will bless us. God is good. God is great. He will give us what we need. All that prevents him from doing so is our doubts. James is not questioning God's power to give but our power to receive. How in the world can we expect to get wisdom from God, if we are foolish enough to doubt him? James echoes the words of Jesus, "Have faith and do not doubt" (Matthew 21:21).

Doubt is not the only hindrance to prayer. Conflict, apathy, and selfishness also can block our way to God.

> Those conflicts and disputes among you, where do they come from? Do they not come from your cravings that are at war within you? You want something and do not have it; so you

> commit murder. And you covet something and cannot obtain it; so you engage in disputes and conflicts. You do not have because you do not ask. You ask and do not receive, because you ask wrongly, in order to spend what you get on your pleasures (4:1-3).

Why is it we do not get what we want from God? One reason, James says, is we do not ask. Why don't we always ask God for what we want? We may realize what we want is not what we truly need. Or perhaps we doubt God's power or desire to help us. Maybe we think we can get what we want without his help. Self-sufficiency gets in the way of prayer. Or the ineffectiveness of our prayers could be due to lack of effort on our part. We simply do not take the time to ask. It is not as though God needs us to ask before he can bless us. He already knows what we need. But for our own sake, we need to ask. We need a reminder that we depend on our Father

Will God give us everything we ask for? No. Not if we ask selfishly for what brings pleasure only to us. God is not a genie in a bottle who grants our wishes. Prayer is not a magical formula for wealth or pleasure. When we pray, we must be careful to ask for what is ultimately good and pleasurable, not for immediate gratification of our desires. We must also pray with the needs and wants of others in mind, not just for what is best for us.

God will give us wisdom and everything else we need, but not necessarily everything we want. He always answers our prayers, although we must sometimes wait for his answer. But the need for trust and patience does not mean that prayer does not work. James assures us that prayer is powerful:

> Are any among you suffering? They should pray. Are any cheerful? They should sing songs of praise. Are any among you sick? They should call for the elders of the church and have them pray over them, anointing them with oil in the name of the Lord. The prayer of faith will save the sick, and the Lord will raise them up; and anyone who has committed sins will be forgiven. Therefore confess your sins to one another, and pray for one another, so that you may be healed.

> The prayer of the righteous is powerful and effective. Elijah was a human being like us, and he prayed fervently that it might not rain, and for three years and six months it did not rain on the earth. Then he prayed again, and the heavens gave rain and the earth yielded its harvest (5:13-18).

James lists several marvelous things God will do for us if we pray for ourselves and for others: he will end our suffering, heal our sickness, and forgive our sins. Prayer to God is beyond a doubt "powerful and effective." Elijah prayed for drought and then for rain as a sign to the Israelites (1 Kings 17:1; 18:1), and God answered his prayers immediately because they were in accordance with his will. We can pray with the same fervor and assurance, knowing our prayers are effective if we pray in God's will.

Questions for further discussion

1. Like Jesus, have you ever prayed with loud cries and tears? Did God answer? Does God answer "yes" to every prayer?
2. Can we pray without doubting? Are we always sure God will give us what we ask? Should we be?
3. Why don't we always ask God for what we want?
4. What prayers are selfish? If we ask for something we want, is that a selfish prayer?
5. Was Elijah really a human being like us? Do we sometimes put biblical characters on too high of a pedestal? How can we avoid that?

CHAPTER TWELVE
DISCIPLINE YOURSELF FOR THE SAKE OF YOUR PRAYERS: PRAYER IN OTHER NEW TESTAMENT BOOKS

Even the neglected books of the New Testament, the shorter epistles and Revelation, have significant teachings on prayer. These books explore the place of prayer in the life of disciples, clearly displaying its power and beauty.

Prayer in 1 Peter (3:7; 4:7)

Peter writes to "the exiles of the Dispersion" to encourage them to be faithful although they must suffer as Jesus did. "Exiles" is a significant term. It implies that these Christians are torn from the prevailing social structure because of their faith in Christ. Now they are citizens of a new holy kingdom and their old companions, surprised at their new behavior, ostracize and even persecute them.

This situation is one for prayer. Peter speaks of prayer in this letter in surprising contexts. Instructing his readers on Christian marriage, he tells wives to accept the authority of their husbands and tells husbands to show consideration for their wives. Following this instruction would, no doubt, promote harmony in the home and set a good example for those outside the church, but these are not the purposes Peter gives for his advice. Instead, wives and husbands are to act this way *"so that nothing may hinder your prayers"*(3:7).

This is the only reference in the New Testament to prayer in marriage (except, perhaps, for 1 Corinthians 7:5), but its off-handed tone implies shared prayer between spouses was taken for granted by early Christians. Trouble between Christian marriage partners is especially disturbing because it gets in the way of their prayers. In today's world, not sleeping together is the sure sign of marital difficulty. To Peter, being unable to pray together is even more devastating to the relationship.

But how often do we pray with those who are dearest to us — our husbands, wives, children? Are we too busy? Do we consider prayer purely a private affair, none of our family's business? Peter will not allow that. He expects his readers to pray together. If we take the Bible seriously, we must make prayer an integral and central part of our married life.

Peter places prayer in marriage, but also with the end of the world: *"The end of all things is near; therefore be serious and discipline yourselves for the sake of your prayers"* (4:7). Christians live in the shadow of the cross and in anticipation of the return of Christ. Most Christians today seem to think little about the end of the world. Even when they do, it usually is in terms of idle speculation about the signs of the times. We do not know when he will return, but we are to believe he will. Each generation of Christians lives in the last days. Each can say, 'Jesus is coming soon."

If we are convinced that his coming is near, our prayer lives are changed. Prayer becomes something more serious, something that is not played at, but that is nurtured in a systematic way. Peter's word is "discipline." Discipline is almost a bad word today. We live in the age of freedom, of excess, of feeling good about ourselves. Discipline conjures up images of monks in their cells, or Marines on Paris Island, or the worst of reform schools. The only place one seems to meet discipline today is in the gym. Many are almost religious about their workouts. "No pain, no gain," they say.

Peter's words remind us something is more important than the health and strength of our bodies, more important than anything in this world. The end of all things is near. Soon all that will be left is the reality of the God we pray to. With that in mind, we would do well to pay more attention to our spiritual discipline than our physical workouts. Discipline in prayer means praying regularly, even when we don't feel like it, praying when it is not convenient, even praying when it hurts. Wrestling with God in prayer can be painful, but as with all discipline, "No pain, no gain." The realization that the end of all things is near motivates us to disciplined prayer.

Prayer in John's Epistles

John repeats a theme found throughout the New Testament – ask and you will receive. The Christian who is clothed with the righteousness of Christ has assurance that God answers prayer: "Beloved, if our hearts do not condemn us, we have boldness before God; and we receive from him whatever we ask, because we obey his commandments and do what pleases him" (1 John 3:21-22).

John's words are similar to those of Jesus, "Whatever you ask for in prayer in faith, you will receive" (Matthew 21:22), and to the advice of James, "But ask in faith, never doubting" (James 1:6). To John, however, the confidence that we will receive what we ask from God is based not on faith, but on obedience. John is not advocating "works righteousness" that demand perfection from Christians, but he, like James, teaches that faith and obedience are inseparable. True faith leads to obedience, and to obey God is "to believe in the name of his Son Jesus Christ and to love one another" (1 John 3:23).

In other words, prayer is part of something much larger; it is Christian prayer only when it involves our entire relationship to God. It is legitimate and right to ask God for what we need, but when we approach him, he must not be a stranger to us. We dare not pray only when we are desperate or have exhausted our own resources or when we, frankly, have nothing better to do. We pray to our Father and as a loving Father, he gives us what we ask. Such a Father deserves and demands our trust and obedience. It is when "our hearts do not condemn us," when we know our relation to our Father is genuine, that we can approach him boldly.

John not only tells us how to pray ("with boldness") but also for whom to pray:

> And this is the boldness we have in him, that if we ask

anything according to his will, he hears us. And if we know that he hears us in whatever we ask, we know we have obtained the requests made of him. If you see your brother or sister committing what is not a mortal sin, you will ask, and God will give life to such a one – to one whose sin is not mortal. There is sin that is mortal; I do not say that you should pray about that. All wrongdoing is sin, but there is a sin that is not mortal (1 John 5:14-17).

Sin is another little-used word in our society, even in the church. In America we believe strongly in the individual's freedom to do whatever he or she wants, "as long as it doesn't hurt anyone." As part of a church, many Christians feel they should mind their own business, saying Christianity is a purely private affair and the foibles of their fellow Christians are strictly between them and God.

The Bible will not allow us the luxury of a strictly private Christianity. Whether we like it or not, we are responsible for each other. Your sins, even when they are not personally against me, are my business, for you are my brother or sister. Oh, yes, my sins are your business, too.

This does not make church member into busybodies, eager to find the latest dirt on others. On the contrary, my concern for your sins should not be to broadcast them or to belittle you, but to hide your sins completely by asking God to forgive them. And when you see me sin, you also are to pray for my forgiveness.

I'm not completely sure what John means about a mortal sin that should not be prayed for. Perhaps any sin we refuse to acknowledge can become a mortal sin. But John clearly challenges us modern Christians to honestly confess our sin and take responsibility for our brothers and sisters. Often in church we put up a false front. Sure, we admit we are sinners (isn't everyone?), but the last thing we would do is to confess a particular sin.

John does not call us to wallow in our sins, to graphically depict our every evil action, but we are to confess them. Even more difficult, we are to care enough for our fellow Christians to confront them with their sins and to pray to

God for them. We may not relish such confrontations, but if we are to be God's children, we must pray for our fellow sinners and accept, even welcome, their prayers for us.

Praying for other Christians is our duty and privilege even when we do not see them sinning. In 3 John, the elder prays for his friend Gaius: *"Beloved, I pray that all may go well with you and that you may be in good health, just as it is well with your soul"*(1:2). We pray for other Christians when they sin. We pray for their health, and most important, we pray for their spiritual health – that it is well with their souls.

Prayer in Revelation

Dragons, beasts with scorpion's tails, plagues on horseback, and jeweled cities fill the pages of John's Apocalypse. No wonder so many people are interested today in the book of Revelation. But while many mine it for hidden clues to the time of the Second Coming, they may miss its more obvious teaching on Christian living. For example, in this final book of the New Testament, we have a most beautiful picture of prayer:

> Another angel with a golden censer came and stood at the altar; he was given a great quantity of incense to offer with the prayers of all the saints on the golden altar that is before the throne. And the smoke of the incense, with the prayers of the saints, rose before God from the hand of the angel
> (8:3-4; see also 5:8).

As the Jews in the Old Testament offered incense to God in the Temple, so we worship God in prayer. Our prayers go up to God as pleasing incense. He wants us to pray. He gladly receives the prayers of the saints. It is appropriate that this is the final word of the New Testament on prayer. Prayer is sublime not because it has some inherent power or because we can pray beautifully. Prayer is sublime because the Lord God Almighty wants us to pray, hears our prayers, and generously blesses. It is not the scent of our offerings that counts, but the glory of the One who receives them.

Questions for further discussion

1. What is the role of prayer in marriage?What can we do to make it more a part of our family life?

2. What are some ways we can discipline ourselves in prayer?

3. What does it mean to pray considering the Second Coming?

4. What does obedience have to do with prayer? Should we not pray for certain disobedient people?

5. Do you most often pray for the physical or the spiritual health of others?

CHAPTER THIRTEEN

CONCLUSION: LORD, TEACH US TO PRAY

What have we learned from this study of prayer in the New Testament? Our quick survey of dozens of biblical passages should not lull us into thinking we are now experts on prayer. But although we still have much to learn, the following lessons are clear.

We Pray to a Powerful and Loving Father

The primary fact of prayer is not the act of prayer, but the One we pray to. Prayer would be a waste of time if addressed to a Deity who did not love us or who could not deliver what he had promised. But our God has all power. His arm is never too short to reach us. Jesus reminds us of this power when he tells us prayer can move mountains. Paul reminds us of this power when he says God can do more than we ask or think. The early church trusted this power to deliver them against impossible odds.

We live in an age of limits, an age where science decides what is possible. Our God is limitless. He stands outside our age and our universe, holding both in his hands. No task is beyond him. No cause too hopeless. No outlook too bleak. Whatever we ask, God can do.

But an all-powerful God is no good to us if he is far away. God is our intimate. Our troubles are his. Good news is ours – God is not only power, he is love. He loved us enough to send his Son. He loves us enough to make us his children. He wants only to bless, to give good gifts.

We don't have to trick this God to bless us. Magical phrases or eternal repetition cannot manipulate him. If we simply speak to our loving Father in faith, his power will be ours.

We Pray with a Loving Savior

When the disciples asked, "Lord, teach us to pray," Jesus gave them what we call the Lord's Prayer. But this is not the only way he teaches us to pray. In all his prayers he shows us the true path of discipleship. As we have seen, he often prayed alone; so should we. He prayed in the rough spots of life; so should we. He prayed not just for himself, but for others. He prayed that the Father's will be done.

But he is more than our example in prayer. He is that, and it is a marvel unbelievable that God not only allows us to pray but he also prays himself in the person of his Son. But Jesus not only models prayer, and he not only prays for us. He prays *with* us. When we pray in his name, we pray like him and with his authority, but what is more, he meets us in prayer. By the Spirit our prayers join with his. He intercedes for us. He makes our prayers his own. If the loving Father hears us as his children, how much more will he hear his beloved Son as he prays with us?

We Are Helped in Prayer by the Holy Spirit

"We do not pray as we ought," Paul says. Thank God we do not have to pray correctly to pray effectively. The effectiveness of our prayers is not dependent on our own abilities. We have help. We have a helper, the Holy Spirit. He intercedes for us, translating our pitiful attempts at expression into ineffable words that touch the heart of the Father. Whenever we pray sincerely and in faith, we pray in the Spirit.

So the heart of Christian prayer lies in the fact that prayer is, from beginning to end, a work of God. God the Father is the object of prayer, the powerful, loving One we pray to. God the Son is our model and companion in prayer. We pray in his name and he prays with us. God the Spirit is our helper in prayer, turning our words into God's words.

This takes the pressure off us in prayer. Yes, we must pray in the right way for the right things. Yes, we must learn to pray. Yes, we must discipline ourselves to pray. But we never pray alone. We have all the help we need.

We Must Learn To Pray

Prayer is not a natural ability. Almost everyone has prayed sometime, but Christian prayer is a learned activity. The disciples knew Jewish prayers. Perhaps John the Bapist taught them to pray, but they still felt the need to learn from Jesus.

How do we learn to pray? Through studies like this one. The Bible teaches us to pray. As we see the biblical men and women wrestle with God in prayer, we imitate their faith. As we watch Jesus pray, we follow his leading.

How do we learn to pray? Through the examples of our fellow Christians. We learn to pray from our mothers and fathers. We learn prayer in church, watching the spiritual giants around us. We pray with them, and before too long we find ourselves praying like them.

How do we learn to pray? Practice, practice, practice. One learns to pray by praying. By praying regularly, even with mixed feelings and our thoughts confused. We build up our praying strength by praying. Prayer teaches prayer.

We Should Pray Alone

At times it is easy to pray – when someone leads a prayer at a meal, at prayer time in church, when someone says, "Let's pray together." What is more difficult is blocking out time for private prayer. Even Jesus had trouble finding time to pray alone. The crowds doggedly hunted for him. To find the time, he awoke early in the morning and stole away from his disciples, or sometimes he stayed awake all night in prayer.

We must find these or other ingenious schemes to make time for private prayer. The greatest obstacle to our prayers is us. It takes a burning desire to pray to move one to lose sleep. There will always be plenty of reasons or excuses for not praying. Just do it. Pray. The promise is that if we do speak to God in our secret room, he will hear and reward us openly.

We Should Pray With Other Christians

Small group prayer is a special blessing from God. When one or more Christians ask us to pray with them, we should always take that opportunity. Something special happens when Christians pray together. We become closer to God and to one another. "Brother" and "sister" become more than church words. What is more, when two or three agree in prayer, Jesus promises to be with them.

Other Christians should be on our mind even when we pray alone. We have the privilege to pray for each other. Jesus prayed for his disciples and for us. Paul prayed for the churches. Prayer is never a selfish act. In prayer we intercede with God for our fellows. Their troubles become ours and then become his.

Praying with and for others also entails asking them to pray for us. Lone Ranger Christianity was never God's plan. When trouble comes we are not to grin and bear it. We are to pray and bear it. And we do not bear it alone. Others help carry our burdens to God. Nothing would revitalize our churches more than a commitment to pray for one another and to ask one another for prayer.

We Should Pray With the Entire Church

Public prayer also has a place. Through the centuries whenever Christians have met together for worship, they invariably have prayed. Liturgical prayers have gained a bad reputation in the eyes of some. In churches with written prayers the danger of insincerely doing things by rote is present. Christ condemns vain repetitions. In churches with spontaneous prayers, the danger of thoughtlessness, flippancy, and pretentious performance is ever-present. Praying for show is also condemned.

In short, public prayer in church is difficult. For the prayer leader there is pressure to say the right thing, to include all in the prayer, and to avoid praying to please people instead of God. For the congregation the struggle to listen and to make the prayer its own can be demanding. We must say, "Amen."

God wills the church to pray together. When the whole church prays, we experience the unity Christ prayed for, "That they all may be one." In prayer we unite with one another and with the Father, Son, and Spirit.

We ShouldCultivate a Habit of Prayer

Habit is a bad word. We usually speak only of bad habits, not good ones. "A habit of prayer" sounds like a contradiction. Is not prayer to be sincere, spontaneous, and heartfelt? If merely a habit, will it not lose its meaning?

Jesus had a habit of prayer. His prayers did not lose their meaning. The early Christians devoted themselves to prayer. Paul prayed constantly. Doing something regularly, even habitually, does not necessarily make it boring and meaningless.

How do we develop a habit of prayer? It takes discipline. It might mean setting aside certain times of the day when, no matter what we are doing, we stop and pray. It might mean sometimes writing out prayers. Whatever technique one uses, the important thing is to pray regularly and often.

We Should Pray in the Crises of Our Lives

Regular prayer is the mark of a Christian disciple. We pray when it is convenient and when it is not. But some times especially call for prayer. When our faith is weak, when illness strikes, when a loved one dies, when death is near, in all the dark valleys of life – moments like these bring us to our knees. It is proper and right to pray when in need. Some Christians mistakenly do not want to bother God with their problems. But he loves us. He doesn't mind being bothered.

When we pray in crises, we do not always know what to pray for. The Spirit will help us. When we pray in pain, we don't know how God will answer. He may remove the problem, no matter how big it is. We know he has the power. He may strengthen us so we can stand the pain. He may point us to the ultimate answer of the resurrection. Whatever his answer, we believe he hears us, and we know his grace is enough for us.

Prayer Is More Than Asking for Things

We have emphasized the power and love of the God who hears our prayers and gives us what we need. But prayer is a much richer experience than merely applying for a blessing. In the New Testament prayer always begins with praise and thanksgiving to God. When we pray, we focus not primarily on our needs and wants but on the holiness and grandeur of our God. He is the Almighty. He alone is God. He alone is worthy of our praise.

This gracious God made us, sustained us, and saved us. It is sheer grace that we stand in his presence. No amount of work can repay him for his love. Our most righteous deeds are filthy rags. When we have done all we can, we still are worthless servants. The one thing we can do is thank him. As Christians our entire lives say thank you to God. Every action praises him. We offer every prayer with thanksgiving.

Thanksgiving, requests, and intercessions are parts of our prayers. Prayer is also communication with God. In prayer we speak, but we also listen. In prayer we come to know God's will and we become one with that will. Prayer energizes our spiritual lives.

Prayer Is Part of a Total Relationship With God

God is no slave to do our bidding. Prayer is not hocus-pocus to make our wishes come true. God is not in our power, we are in his. We dare not come to him only when we feel like it. Our prayers must reflect the whole of our life of obedience.

God wants us to pray. He wants us to ask him for what we need. But he really wants us, not our prayers. He demands all of us. Prayer, then, is not the only time we show our spirituality. All of life is our prayer to God. Working, playing, praying, sleeping, studying, caring — all are prayers if done to his glory.

There are special times called prayer, times when alone or with our brothers and sisters we bow before our Father. Yet prayer must not be an interruption in our lives. It should flow from our faith and our acts of service. Prayer is not just a righteous act. It is the act of one made righteous by the blood of Christ.

Studying About Prayer Is Different from Praying

We end with a warning. Now that we know what the New Testament teaches about prayer, we dare not return to our old prayer life. Quoting Scriptures on prayer is not praying. Knowledge without action is vain. Faith without works is dead. If we really believe what the New Testament says on prayer, only one course is open to us. We must pray, pray more, pray longer, and pray differently. Our Father is there to hear us. Our Savior is there to pray with us. The Spirit is there to help us.

Let us pray.

Questions for further discussion

1. Does prayer work? Is it better to say God works when we pray?
2. If prayer becomes a habit, does it begin to lose its meaning?
3. Should we ever be reluctant to pray in a crisis? What does it say about us if that is the only time we pray?
4. What is the most life-changing thing you learned in this study of prayer?
5. What are some specific ways your prayer life has changed because of this study?

Printed in the United States
50651LVS00003B/182